# Love Is an Open Door

D0878723

# LOVE IS
# AN OPEN
# DOOR

---•◦•---

## by Bill Bair

## WITH GLENN D. KITTLER

Steward Press
25 Turner Drive, Chappaqua, New York 10514

*Library of Congress Cataloging in Publication Data*

Bair, Bill.
    Love is an open door.

    1. Bair, Bill.  2.  Bair Foundation.  3.  Church
work with juvenile delinquents.  4.  Children—
Institutional care—New Wilmington, Pa.  I.  Kittler,
Glenn D.  II.  Title.
BR1725.B3314A33        248'.2 [B]        73-17023
ISBN 0-912376-07-4

Copyright© 1974 by William J. Bair

All rights reserved
Printed in the United States of America

*To* Walter Allan Bair
and
Mary Keith Bair

To recognize any *one* of hundreds of people who influenced my life over the years would be an inexcusable disservice to all of the others who also graciously excused my short-comings and encouraged my faltering faith.

My father, Walter Allan Bair, died April 28, 1969. My mother, Mary Keith Bair, is now seventy-nine and still takes me to task when I get too big for my britches.

For giving me the privilege of being their son, I shout with the deepest of sincerity, "Praise the Lord!"

# Foreword

We exchanged glances. We'd been with this fellow fifteen minutes and this was the third time he'd thrown wide his arms and let out a window-rattling "Praise the Lord!"

We'd come out to New Wilmington, Pennsylvania, to interview Bill Bair for *Guideposts* magazine, and while we were impressed with what we saw—this warm and welcoming house, a front door that never closed, and some of the happiest young faces we'd ever laid eyes on—still, stock phrases made us nervous. One of *those,* the glance we gave each other said: one of those Christians who repeat certain words so often they cease to have meaning.

Two days and about a hundred Praise the Lords later, we'd changed our minds. We'd gotten to know Marilyn Bair, Bill's wife and the loving center of this busy household. We'd talked to the kids who lived here, kids who'd arrived confused, angry, drug-addicted, at odds with their schools, their parents, and themselves—and stayed to become the radiant and purposeful young people we were meeting. We'd visited some of the other families who are sharing in Bill and Marilyn's ministry to "kids who need a place to go." And we'd discovered that praising the Lord wasn't a phrase with Bill at all; it was simply a description of what's going on in New Wilmington.

We'd discovered, too, that we'd run across more than a magazine article. We had glimpsed a solution to the problems of young people today so enormous in its potential that it would take a book to tell it right.

And so, a little while later, Bill came to our house in the suburbs of New York. The purpose of the trip was for Bill to meet Glenn Kittler, the man we hoped would write the book. At least, that was our purpose. For Bill the point to every day, no matter where he is or why, is kids, and so he set out to meet the teen-agers in the neighborhood.

"Look, Bill," we cautioned him, "this isn't New Wilmington. These are sophisticated kids around here; you have to be subtle. For heaven's sake don't go around asking people if they love Jesus." We'd been talking with three young people in the area (subtly, of course) and we didn't want Bill's old-fashioned approach scaring them off.

It didn't. All three of them showed up at our house that evening, along with twenty-seven others. Bill had gone around asking people if they loved Jesus and they said, "No, tell us about Him."

We have a theory about people who work together on a book. We think they should be as unlike as possible. (Maybe that's why we've found our man-woman collaboration a good balance.) Two people with the same background and viewpoint can fall into a kind of closed-circuit communication that leaves a lot of people out. That's why we knew Glenn

Kittler was the ideal person to help Bill set down his experiences. Here would be no private code. Glenn the urbane New Yorker, Bill with SMALL TOWN stamped from his vocabulary to his choice of socks. Glenn the grateful bachelor, Bill the family man for whom less than twelve around the dinner table is a solitary snack. Glenn the scholarly Roman Catholic, Bill who doesn't care what the label on the outside of the church is, so long as the hymn singing's loud and lively. Two men alike only in their lack of sentimentality and their love of God.

As we had known they would, Glenn and Bill liked each other at once and we waited with excitement for the book that would result. When it came, we read through it almost fearfully. How could you pin down on paper the life that pulses through those homes in Pennsylvania? But here it was: the parents and the kids, the heartaches and the triumphs. Here was Bill himself, life-sized and natural. Bill struggling and balking, Bill resisting the tug of God on his life. And then—Bill obeying. And through this obedience, learning day by day the lessons every one of us needs to know, whatever the job God has given us to do.

For beyond Bill and Marilyn, beyond the young people and their families, there is Someone else on these pages. Essentially, it is a book about Him: what He does, what He asks, what He gives—a book that makes you want to say, well, you know, stock phrase or not,

Praise the Lord!

JOHN AND ELIZABETH SHERRILL

Love Is an Open Door

# 1

"John," I told him, "you're making a big mistake. I can understand your wanting a son, but why don't you and Bea adopt a baby? Don't take this fourteen-year-old kid into your home. You have your three little girls to think of."

In the tone he used when he was being patient with me, John said, "Bea and I didn't come out here for advice, Bill. We've made up our minds. We just came to ask Marilyn for her prayers."

I looked at my wife. She was beaming. She said, "It will go all right, John, if you love him enough."

Bea Love said, "We do, Marilyn. So will you."

I noticed that John Love hadn't asked for my prayers. My wife's brother didn't think I was much of a Christian. But that wasn't fair; I said my prayers, I went to church. All right, maybe I wasn't on fire for Jesus Christ and for the Bible, the way John was, the way Bea and Marilyn were. But as far as I was concerned I was as good a Christian as anybody else. At the moment, I was a lot more concerned about the ruffian they were about to take into their home as a foster child.

"John, you've said yourself that the kid swears like a drunken sailor. Do you want your daughters to hear that kind of language?"

"That will stop when he feels secure," John said.

"What about his stealing?"

"I'm not worried about that, either."

"What about his fights? And his vandalism? And all those times he's run away?" I pointed out. "What makes you think he'll stay with you?"

"Would you stay where you're not wanted?"

"All right," I conceded, "the kid has had a tough life and he should be helped. But at fourteen he's too old to get any help in a foster home. He should be put into some kind of institution where at least they can control him. It's not the boy that I'm against. It's his age. It's too late to change him."

John glanced at his watch. "Bea, we promised the baby-sitter we'd be home by nine."

Marilyn and I walked with the Loves to their car. John and Marilyn kissed good night; then Bea and Marilyn kissed. Public displays of affection had always made me feel uncomfortable. I just said good night to them both. They got into the car.

John said, "Remember, Marilyn—prayers."

My wife smiled and nodded. "Without ceasing."

As we watched them drive away, I lit a cigarette. "Those two are asking for a heap of trouble," I said.

"So are you, Bill Bair," Marilyn replied. She took the cigarette out of my hand, let it drop to the sidewalk, and stepped on it. She was always doing something like that.

"The trouble with you, Bill, is that you won't give the boy a chance."

We'd had coffee on the back porch, so I helped Marilyn gather up the cups and take them into the kitchen. As Marilyn began rinsing the china, I went to the refrigerator for the bottle of beer I had brought home from the tavern where I usually stopped for a few beers after work. It wasn't there. I glanced at the garbage pail and saw the empty bottle. I asked, "Honey, did you throw the beer down the sink again?"

"I certainly didn't drink it," she said. She was always doing something like that, too. I had to watch her every minute.

Marilyn and I had been married over a year and we were both eager for a child. But by that I meant a child of our own. I knew I could never do what John Love was about to attempt. Of course, under certain circumstances I would be willing to adopt an infant. But a fourteen-year-old boy already set in his ways—and evil ways at that—this was something I just could not do. And I didn't think anybody else should.

Sunday, John and Bea and their three girls went and got Charles and brought him back to our town of Altoona, Pennsylvania, where we'd all lived all our lives. Marilyn and I gave them some time to get settled and then went over. There was a lot of excitement in the house as we let ourselves in. The girls were showing Charles around the place. They introduced him to us.

I disliked the kid on sight. He was small for his age, maybe four feet, nine inches tall, and skinny. His dark hair looked like a doormat on a muddy day. He needed a bath. His clothes would have been rejected by charitable organizations. He wore glasses. He just glanced at Marilyn when she was introduced as his aunt. He did not stand up or make any effort to shake hands with me when I was identified to him as his uncle. He was sullen, silent and, I felt, mean. But the Loves treated him like a king. You'd think he was some sort of a Christmas present. The three girls were all talking to him at once. John and Bea couldn't take their eyes off him.

After a while, the girls went into the kitchen to start making toasted cheese sandwiches for lunch, and the rest of us went to the dining-room table. In a few minutes, Joan, the middle girl, came in with four sandwiches on a platter. Usually Marilyn and I were served first at the Loves' house. This time, Joan went first to Charles. He put three of the sandwiches on his plate. I was ready to break his arm. But when I saw the way he gulped them down, I figured maybe he hadn't eaten for a while.

There was a piano in the room. Janie, the oldest daughter, was taking lessons, and she played for us. In an unexpected show of life, Charles got up and drifted over to the piano and stood there watching Janie's hands as though this were something he was seeing for the first time.

During the whole visit, the children were too near for us to have much of a chance to talk. Finally the time came to leave. John and Bea accompanied Marilyn and me to our car. When we were away from the house, I asked, "Well, what do you think?"

John said, "Charles?"

"Yes."

"He'll be all right."

"He doesn't have much to say for himself."

"It's his first day."

I could hear the telephone ringing in the house. "He could use a bath," I said.

Bea laughed. "Yes. That's first. I'm going to have him in the tub in fifteen minutes."

"He needs clothes," John said. "We'll take him downtown tomorrow and outfit him."

The door opened and Charles came out and called, "Hey, Dad, you're wanted on the phone."

The big smile that hit John's face almost sliced his head off. He looked at the boy and answered, "All right, son. I'll be right there." He looked at us. His face was all lit up. I couldn't remember ever seeing him so happy. He said, "Come for supper some night this week." And he hurried into the house.

I thought, "Dad," already. The first day. I couldn't decide whether Charles was just a terribly lonely boy who finally got what he wanted or if he was the con artist of all time. But I knew that John had certainly gotten what he wanted.

Marilyn had always been close to her family, just as I was to mine, and so there was a great deal of visiting back and forth. As the months passed, I couldn't make up my mind how I felt about Charles. John told me that he was being no more trouble than the average boy. Sometimes he was a little lazy, sometimes a little slow, sometimes a little rebellious. But he seemed to react favorably to the same discipline that the girls received when they acted up. Charles was holding his own at school, although he was a couple of years behind his age group. He was going to church and he took part in the family's evening prayers without any recognizable reaction. He was being a boy.

But there was one thing about him that I found disconcerting. He had a habit of touching John on practically any occasion. No matter where we all happened to be, Charles would find a reason to ask John something. As he spoke, he'd touch him on the arm, on the chest, around the shoulders. I noticed, too, that John returned the touches, squeezing the boy's shoulder, scratching his back, brushing his hair out of his eyes. I could never get used to that. As a boy, I never doubted that my father loved me, but the only times we had physical contact were when he walloped me. When I grew older, we shook hands a few times. In my whole life, I had kissed my mother three times—the day I left home to join the navy, the day I got back, and the day I got married. We just were not a demonstrative family. My folks were of Pennsylvania-Dutch stock, and though we all had good times together we never made much of a show out of it.

But the Loves lived up to their name, touching and kissing practically every time they were close enough for contact. I had discussed this with Marilyn early in our courting days, and after that I was excluded from these family displays. As time went on, they bothered me less and less, until Charles showed up. A boy's need for affection from his father was something I could not understand. I thought this touching business between John and Charles was strange. A few times when we were within reach of each other, Charles would touch my hand or my arm. I always found a way to retreat. The boy puzzled me.

A year passed. The Reverend Leroy Harrison, pastor of the Methodist church we all usually attended, announced that he would be holding a week's revival. I knew without being told that Marilyn would want to attend every night and I was prepared to take her, although I felt that seven successive nights were a lot more church than I needed. Every night there was an altar call. Every night, I could sense that Marilyn, sitting beside me, was praying that I would go forward and accept Christ. I refused to budge: I felt that I had already accepted Christ in my own way, and I wasn't going to make a spectacle of myself about it, even for my wife.

One night the services were addressed mainly to the teen-agers who were present. Then the altar call was given. Several teen-agers got up and went forward. I whispered to Marilyn, "This is foolish. These kids don't know what they're doing. It will never last."

Another figure came from behind and caught my eye. It was Charles.

If the boy puzzled me before, he now absolutely bewildered me. I had no idea what changes to look for in him now that he had become a Christian, and I didn't observe any. John and Bea reported that he had become more loving, more outgoing, more a part of the family, the church, the community. Well, fine, I thought, but he sure wasn't any different toward me—still a bit cool, distant, quiet.

One night the Loves were coming over for supper. I had wanted to get off from work early so that I could get home in time to mow the lawn, but one thing led to another on the job, and I got home even later than I usually did. I went right to work on the grass. The day had been hot, and now the setting sun seemed aimed directly at me. I wasn't half finished when the Loves pulled up.

As they got out of the car I called, "Go out to the back porch. Marilyn should have the coffee ready."

They all headed for the porch. Suddenly Charles turned and came toward me. As he neared, he brought up his hands, and I wondered if he was going to touch me.

Instead, he took hold of the lawn mower handle. "Let me finish this for you, Uncle Bill." He turned his back on me and pushed the mower away at a fast pace.

I watched him, stunned. It was more than his helpful gesture. He had called me Uncle Bill. All along, we had managed to exchange idle conversation without his giving me any label at all. Now I was Uncle Bill. I liked it. I felt good. I wondered if this was the way John Love had felt the first time Charles had called him Dad. Suddenly I could understand that it was a man-making experience to be loved by a boy. I almost wished there was a boy around who would call me Dad.

Little did I know how dangerous even a half wish can be.

# 2

My parents had five children and I gave them more headaches than the other four combined. My father was a quiet
man who enjoyed his evening newspaper. He had his favorite chair in the dining room, near the register through which
the heat came up from the basement. While he read and
Mother sewed, the kids settled down to their homework—
all except me. I was never much of a student. I flunked first
grade, which some people think is impossible to do. I also
flunked fourth grade. I often wondered if I was really related
to these serious, capable people.

We were poor, but then everybody was poor in those
days. My father worked forty-five years for the Pennsylvania
Railroad, but during the depression he was laid off. He took
a job as a hand on the Rossman farm in Center County,
almost fifty miles away, which was a long trip in those days.
For almost two years, Dad would leave home on Sunday
night to go out to the farm and we would not see him again
until the next Saturday evening. It was a bad time. I can

remember, when I was six, going to the mountains to pick huckleberries with my brother and sisters. We sold the berries for seven cents a quart to an aunt who had a restaurant in town. It was the only spending money we had.

I told my parents that we would be able to bring more berries down from the mountains if we had a wagon to carry the containers. I hoped this would inspire my father to buy us a wagon, but I was mistaken. "That's a good idea," said Dad. "Save up for one." And so I did. Whenever money came in from berries or chores I did for neighbors, I put the coins in a tin container which Mother kept on the top shelf of the kitchen cabinet, out of reach of temptation.

At last the day came when there was enough to order the wagon from Shaffer's store. He had to send to Pittsburgh for it, which meant more waiting. Finally, when I got home from school one day, Mother told me that the store had called. The wagon was at the train station, would be taken to the store, and then would be delivered in a day or two. I couldn't wait. I ran the few blocks to the store. Standing in front of Shaffer's was a horse-drawn freight cart, on it a small red wagon that had to be mine. It was love at first sight.

I ran into the store. "Deacon, is that my wagon out there?"

"It's all yours," he said.

I rushed back just as the delivery men were lowering the wagon to the sidewalk. "It's mine," I said. "Deacon said I could take it." When I took the handle in my hand for the first time, I went weak with joy. Years later, getting my first car didn't thrill me so much. I stood there staring at that wagon in wonder, as though it were something that had just been born. That evening, my folks let me keep it in the living room, where I could watch it.

I took the wagon everywhere I went. I used old license plates to make fenders for the wheels, and Dad brought me a lantern from Rossman's farm for a headlight. Grandma Bair's house stood on a steep hill. I don't know how many times I climbed it and went roaring down it in the wagon. One day I realized that the trip down stirred up an impressive amount of dust. I decided to stir up even more by tying a burlap bag to the rear axle. I was having so much fun that I never noticed Grandma Bair's weekly wash hanging on the line in her yard.

As I was rattling past Grandma's house in yet another cloud of dust, she came running out, waving and hollering, and I knew I was in trouble. There were some bushes at the end of the run and I ducked into them. She dragged me out and gave me a good clip on the head, the only time she ever hit me. Then she said, "Now, we're going to sit on my front porch until your father gets here." It was forty-five minutes until Dad arrived, and then I wasn't able to sit again for two days.

Another adventure in transportation also ended in disaster. My brother Allan got a bicycle. I was dying to have a bike of my own, but my parents told me I was too young and too small. They wouldn't even let Allan ride me on his crossbar, saying that this was too dangerous.

One Sunday morning the craving to ride Allan's bicycle got too strong for me. Allan and my sisters had already left for Sunday school and I was waiting to walk to church with my parents. Then the idea struck. I said to my father, "Dad, instead of waiting for you, I guess I'll just go ahead." I left the house and ran to the corner, then turned into an alley and hid. A few minutes later, I watched my parents walking to church. As soon as my folks were out of sight, I headed directly for Allan's bicycle in the garage. Soon I was making my way up and down the streets of the neighborhood, free and fast, convinced that I had wings.

I came upon my cousin Jimmy Kyper and called, "Come on, Jimmy, let me take you for a ride." He said okay, and climbed up on the crossbar. Off we went, laughing and shouting. Suddenly Jimmy moved on the crossbar, and his left heel tangled in the front wheel spokes. The bike skidded to a halt. I went flying over Jimmy's head and landed hard on the macadam road. I'll never forget how I hollered. My arm was bleeding. I looked at Jimmy. His foot was trapped in the spokes and was so badly bent I was sure it was broken.

Finally a woman heard my howls and came out of her house. She helped me to my feet and we ran over to Jimmy. He was in too much pain to holler. We tried to get his foot out of the wheel, but every time we touched him he moaned. The woman went into her house to get her husband and the man came out with a pair of wire cutters. I stopped worrying about Jimmy's foot and began to be scared for the bike. Every time the man cut another spoke, I pleaded, "That's enough!" He had to cut over a dozen spokes before Jimmy's foot was free. Jimmy tried to get up but couldn't stand without help.

"Is there somebody we can call who's got a car?" the woman asked.

My folks were at church, but Jimmy's father was home, and he had a car. He arrived in a few minutes, worried at first; but when he saw that Jimmy's foot was not broken he began to get angry. He drove us to my house. The front wheel of the bike was so badly hooked that I had to hang out the side window and hold the bike up off the ground as we drove. We'd been home about ten minutes when my family returned. First my father heard me out, then he said, "All right. First, I'll fix your arm. Then I'm going to fix you. And then you'll have to figure out a way to get Allan's bicycle fixed." Things were fixed in that order.

Mother decided that if I had something constructive to do with my time I might not get into so much trouble. One day she said to me, "Bill, I want you to take piano lessons." The teacher was a woman who lived on Second Avenue, about two miles away, and the lessons cost a dollar. Mother took me there for my first lesson, to meet the teacher; the second time I went alone. As I started out for the third lesson, I thought the whole thing over and came to the conclusion that I would never become a pianist and that the dollar could be better spent some other way. I invited three friends to go to the movies with me, and there was enough cash left for candy all around after the show.

When I got home Mother asked, "Well, what did your music teacher have to say?"

"She told me I'm doing real good."

"What new songs did she give you?"

"She just told me to practice the old ones."

The next Saturday, when I would ordinarily have had my fourth lesson, the dollar went for movies and candy again. But before the fifth lesson, the teacher ran into Mother downtown and asked, "Is Bill sick? I've missed him."

That night I couldn't have sat down to practice even if I wanted to.

The next Saturday, I went to the teacher for what should have been my fifth lesson but was actually my third. I must have done very poorly. The lady asked, "What's the matter, Bill? Haven't you been practicing?" I told her no—our piano was broken. Before I got home, the teacher telephoned my mother with the name of a good repairman. So we had another stormy night in the Bair home.

I could never explain to my parents, or even to myself, why I did these things. Maybe, as our minister kept warning me, it was the company I kept. My closest friend when I was nine and ten years old was Georgie White. Georgie lived a few blocks away in a house that was always damp and cold. At our house, Dad left for work at half-past six, so we were all up and at breakfast by six. This gave me two hours before I was due at school, so I usually headed for Georgie's place. I would let myself in—no one locked their doors in those days —and go upstairs and wake Georgie. His mother had to work and was always gone by the time I got there. Then I'd go out and scrounge around for wood to make a fire in the kitchen stove so that the room would be a bit warmer when he came down to wash.

Georgie did not have breakfast at home. Mrs. White always left a few coins on the kitchen table and, when Georgie was ready, we'd make the ten-minute walk to St. John's Grocery Store. On the way, we had to cross the road on which the streetcar ran up the hill to the cemetery. Whenever we saw a stopped car, we'd sneak up behind it and pull the rope, disconnecting the trolley from the overhead cable. Then we'd run while the conductor jumped from the car and hurled stones at us. We thought this was a grand way to start the day.

Breakfast for Georgie consisted of soft drinks, cookies, and candy. He ate right in the store, and while he was eating lined up his unauthorized menu for lunch. Sometimes he stole a can of tuna fish or baked beans or canned meat, sometimes fruit or pastry. We were experimenting with smoking at the time, so he also stole cans of Sir Walter Raleigh tobacco. At first, watching Georgie steal scared me sick, but I gradually hardened to it and eventually joined him at it.

From time to time, Mr. St. John would catch us stealing. He'd punish us by making us sweep out the store or put new stock on the shelves. This was a mistake on his part. Being able to move around the store, we were able to help ourselves to better booty than he kept up by the door. The store had rats, so Mr. St. John had a cat. This cat was nowhere near as surefooted as cats are supposed to be, and as he made his way along the shelves and over the counters he was always knocking things to the floor. Whatever it was, Mr. St. John would throw out. Once we caught on to this we'd send out a series of cries: "Hey, Mr. St. John, the cat is licking a bottle of milk," or, "Mr. St. John, the cat is playing in the pickle barrel." Looking back, I'm surprised we didn't bankrupt that good man.

When my teacher realized how friendly I was with Georgie White, she spoke to my mother about it. Mother said she didn't understand why I couldn't find nicer boys to play with. I could find "nicer" boys, of course; I had a lot of cousins. I also knew Georgie had no friends but me. I couldn't have said why this made a difference to me. Certainly I couldn't have known I was learning things that would help me with other social outcasts many years later. I only knew I liked him and wanted to be with him. I was eleven when the event occurred which I looked on ever after as a turning point. At school, having flunked first and fourth grades, I was already two years behind my age group when I started fourth grade again—and it was only on a trial basis. I was put into the *D* group, a section for the slow learners. I was so used to failure by now that I had stopped trying: I considered myself a hopeless case. Even when my sisters quizzed me at home until I knew every answer on an upcoming test, the second I picked up my pencil in class my mind went blank. It was useless.

I'd been in fourth grade again about two months when my teacher began to think about sending me back to third. She talked it over with my mother and Mother said that the teacher must do what she felt was best.

But before the change was actually made, our class had a visitor. The district superintendent of schools for East End was a man named Smith. Three or four times a year, Mr. Smith sat in on every class in the district, spending an hour or so in each room appraising the teacher and the students. He seemed to know every kid by name, and how well or, in my case, how badly each kid was doing. To me, Mr. Smith was a man of awesome importance who held my life, at least my scholastic life, in his hands.

This particular morning, Mr. Smith arrived about ten minutes before we were going to take a test. I forget what the subject was; I'm sure I wasn't prepared for it, anyway, and at the sight of Mr. Smith any stray scraps of knowledge fled.

For a few minutes, Mr. Smith stood in the front of the room talking with the teacher. Then he said, "Well now, why don't you get started on the test? I'll just stroll around the room and see how things are going."

I didn't like that, and I began to sweat. The teacher got the list of questions from her desk and began to ask them one by one. Ordinarily, when I didn't know the answer to a question I didn't write anything down at all: I didn't see the sense in writing down something that was probably wrong anyway. But I couldn't just sit there doing nothing in front of Mr. Smith. So, as the questions were asked, I bent over the paper before me and started writing. Without looking at him, I was very much aware of Mr. Smith as he moved up and down the aisles, looking over kids' shoulders. He reached my aisle. When he came to me, I felt his presence sending flames through me. I had already covered two sheets of paper and was starting on a third. Mr. Smith picked up the two sheets and looked over them. Then he looked at what I was writing. He put the papers down and moved on. I only half heard the teacher's next question, but I kept on writing, writing. Finally the test was over and the papers were collected. I didn't know what to do with myself, so I just sat there looking at my hands.

Then I heard Mr. Smith say, "I think Bill Bair deserves a second chance to improve himself. Let's put him in the *C* section."

I looked up. The teacher was so surprised that she took a step backward. She surveyed the *C* section for an empty seat, and when she turned to me I could see the disbelief on her face. She said, "Bill, why don't you take that seat in the second row, behind Marion?"

I couldn't speak. My face felt hot. I gathered my things together and went over to the designated seat. I had spent so much time in the *D* section during my school years that when I glanced around now I found myself surrounded by strangers. The room seemed awfully quiet. Mr. Smith and the teacher were talking again.

Then Mr. Smith faced the class. "Well, children, you're all doing fine work. I'll come to see you again. Good-bye."

Everybody else said good-bye. I couldn't say a word.

At noon, I rushed home like the kid who just found out he had no cavities. "Mom! Mom! Mr. Smith put me in the *C* section!"

Mother was at the stove, putting the finishing touches on the midday meal. "What?" she asked.

"It's true, Mom. Mr. Smith visited our class today and he told the teacher to put me into the *C* section, and she did."

"You've never been in the *C* section in your life."

"I know," I said, "but I am now."

"What happened? What did you say? What did you do?"

"I didn't say anything and I didn't do anything," I said. "Mr. Smith told the teacher, 'I think Bill Bair deserves a second chance.' And the teacher moved me over."

I couldn't talk about anything else. As soon as I finished lunch, I rushed back to school and I had been sitting in my new seat for fifteen minutes when the bell rang and the other kids came in. After school, Georgie was waiting for me, and he asked what I wanted to do that afternoon. I said, "I can't do anything. I've got too much homework." I was more surprised to be saying it than he was to hear it.

As I entered the house Mother said, "If you're going out to play, change your clothes."

I said, "I can't go out. I've got too much homework."

I still remember her look of astonishment as I passed her and headed for my room.

I told everybody who came into the house. I told everybody everywhere I went. My father was working at the Rossman farm at this time and I couldn't wait until Saturday to tell him, so I wrote him a letter.

I wish I could report now that after I was put into the *C* section I became a good student. I didn't. School continued to be difficult for me, but I was willing now to do the extra work I had to do to keep up with the others. For the rest of my years at school, I was always in the *C* section.

I don't know why Mr. Smith decided to give me that chance. As I recall, I didn't even pass the test. Maybe my effort to look busy convinced him that I was at last applying myself. I know that I did apply myself from then on. Being given a second chance to make something better out of myself somehow changed me.

Years later, when I began to work with young people who, for one reason or another, felt that they were doomed to be "*D* section" material for life, I observed the same change in them when they finally realized they were being offered another chance. Another chance was all they wanted, even when, like me, they didn't know it.

# 3

Junior high school helped me to make two discoveries. I discovered that I liked football and I discovered that I liked girls. Football was a natural outgrowth of a game we boys played in our last year at grammar school. At the back of each classroom was a cloakroom where we had to go half a dozen times a day either to hang up our wraps or get them out. Whichever way we were going, the boys would split into two teams, one side trying to block the other from leaving. Being two years behind, I was older and bigger than the other boys in my class, so whichever side I was on always won. I liked it so much that when I entered junior high school I went out for football. Our playing field was adjacent to the railroad tracks, in a town where railroading was the major industry. The field was covered with cinders. Sometimes the air was so thick with smoke from the engines that, on a long pass, the ball would vanish into a low cloud, and we'd all have to stand there waiting for it to reappear before we could burst into action again.

The girl I met one Sunday afternoon at an ice-cream party in Greenwood, a few miles from East End. I noticed her sitting by herself, not much in a party mood, I thought. I also thought she was very pretty, so I went over and started to talk. The girl's name was Martha Sanders. She had been ill, she said, and was still feeling low; she had come to the party only because her mother said she ought to get out of the house and be with young people for a while.

As the party ended I asked, "Martha, can I walk you home?"

"You'd better not," she said. "My mother doesn't like me to be alone with a boy."

"You need company," I reminded her. "Your mother said so."

"All right, then," she said.

There were two ways to Martha's house: the short way, down the road, and the long way, across a field. We chose the field. When we reached Martha's house, her mother was waiting in the doorway.

"Martha, where have you been? You're late."

"We got talking," Martha began, weakly.

Without looking at me, Mrs. Sanders said, "Didn't I tell you I don't want you to be with boys?"

"I'm sorry, Mrs. Sanders," I said. "Martha didn't want me to walk her home. But I could see she wasn't feeling well, and I thought maybe she shouldn't be alone."

Mrs. Sanders looked at me in stern appraisal. "Who are you?"

"Bill Bair."

"Where do you live?"

"In Altoona," I said, careful not to specify the East End.

"You go to church?"

"Oh, yes, ma'am."

"You're not a Holy Roller, are you?"

I could tell she didn't want me to be. "Oh, no, ma'am. We're Salem Reformed."

She thought about it, then said, "Come in and have some lemonade."

Martha Sanders was my girl for seven years. We didn't date, in the usual sense of the word. Nobody had any money in those days. But people gave parties of all kinds, and churches were social centers, so there was always something to do. Sometimes Martha and I just went for a walk, and her mother often had chores for me. We were too young to think about marriage but, had anybody asked me, I suppose I would have said that I was going to marry Martha Sanders.

Louie Morgan, a good friend of mine from high school, also lived in Greenwood. We were about the same age and, although Louie was ahead of me in school, we hung around together. In 1943, Louie turned seventeen, got a driver's license, and started driving the family car to school. It was a 1932 Chrysler, big as a bus. During Easter vacation that year a bunch of us piled into it and went down to Newport News, Virginia, for three days. I came back feeling like a world traveler.

A few days later I noticed, when Louie picked me up for school, that he was upset about something. When he didn't say anything for a while, I finally asked, "What's eating you, Louie?"

"Aw," he said, "I had a fight with my folks last night."

"What about?"

"There's a war going on," Louie said, as though I didn't

know. "Last night, I asked my folks if I could join the navy, and they said no. They want me to finish out the semester and graduate.

"That means three months," Louie went on. "In three months I could finish my boot camp and be out on sea duty." He already sounded like a sailor. "I've thought this over and I know what I'm going to do."

"What?"

He looked at me, his eyes full of schemes. "Do you know that if you're seventeen you can join the navy without having to get your folks' okay?"

I couldn't believe it. "You wouldn't do that, Louie."

"Yes, I would," he said. "I am."

"Wow."

"What about you?"

I looked at him. "What?"

He was beaming. "Join the navy with me, Bill. We'll win the war together. C'mon, Bill. It'll be a lot of fun."

"Gosh, Louie, I don't know," I said. "I haven't thought about it. I figured I'd register when I'm eighteen and then just take what comes along."

"And you'll get garbage," said Louie, getting angry. "If you join the navy, you can choose your duty. I'm getting onto an aircraft carrier."

That sounded exciting, but I still felt uncertain. I said, "I don't like the idea of not telling my folks."

Louie exploded. "If you tell your folks, they'll say no, just like mine. C'mon, Bill. Let's go down to the post office right now and sign up. Or are you chicken?"

"I'm not chicken."

"I'll bet you a dollar that you are."

"I'll bet you a dollar that I'm not," I said. "But I'm still sixteen. I won't be seventeen for three days, on the ninth."

He laughed. "Then let's join up on your birthday, chicken."

"Okay," I said, taking the dare. "Just be sure you have your dollar ready."

For three days, I couldn't think of anything else. I knew I was going to go ahead with it, but I was worried and I was scared. Louie and I had agreed not to tell anybody about it, to keep it from getting back to our families, so I didn't even tell Martha Sanders. I couldn't study. I couldn't eat. I couldn't sleep.

On the morning of my birthday, I left the house as though I was going straight into combat. Louie didn't say much as we drove to school; some other kids were in the car, anyway. I didn't see Louie all day, but we met at his car after school and we went down to the post office. At the door, I said, "Okay, Louie, give me the dollar." He gave me the dollar and we went inside. We went into the room where the navy was accepting enlistments and we told the petty officer in charge that we wanted to join. He asked us a few questions, gave us some forms to fill out, and showed us where to wait for the physical examination. My name was called first, and I passed the physical without any problems. While Louie was being examined, the petty officer swore me into the navy and told me to report back to the post office at 9 A.M. on April 12. I'd be sent to Pittsburgh, he said, where I'd be outfitted and classified. When he dismissed me with a nod, I didn't know whether or not I should salute him, so I just said thanks and went out into the hall to wait for Louie.

When Louie came out, his face was a thunderstorm. He was still adjusting his clothes. He didn't look at me as he walked past. I grabbed his arm and stopped him. "Louie, what's the matter?"

He said, "I flunked the physical."

I couldn't believe my ears. "You flunked the physical?"

"Yeah," he said glumly. "I've got a heart murmur. I probably won't even get into the army now."

So there I was. A year older. A dollar richer. And in the navy. Alone.

It was around five when I got home. Dad was in his favorite chair in the dining room, reading the paper. Mother was in the living room, seated on a stool I had made in junior high school, her rug braiding in her lap. At the time, my brother Allan was in the army, in Panama, and my older sister Elda was a WAVE, studying nursing at Bellevue Hospital in New York. On the way home, I had decided to wait until we were all together at supper—my parents and my younger sisters—to break the news. That way, the family could react all at once and get it over with. But the minute I stepped through the door my news burst out of me.

"Mother—Dad—I have something to tell you. I just joined the navy."

Mother looked sharply at me, then burst into tears.

Dad shot to his feet and glared at me. "What! You big shot, you just think you know it all, don't you?"

Dad sat down and went back to his paper. Mother tried to question me through her sobs. I didn't want anybody to know that I had joined the navy on a dare, so I made a patriotic little speech and said I felt it was something I had to do. When there was nothing left to discuss, Mother went out to the kitchen and started supper and I went upstairs to my room. My sisters came in, then I heard their sobs as they ran up the stairs and into my room, throwing their arms around me. I began to wonder how long it would be before the gold star was hanging in the window.

The navy doctor had told me that I needed some dental work, which he advised me to have done by my own dentist. Mother went with me to the dentist, and when she told him I was about to go into the navy he said he wouldn't charge us. Then Mother and I did something we had never done before. We went to a restaurant for supper. The restaurant was owned by my Aunt Nora, my father's sister, who had been my best customer for the mountain berries I picked. Aunt Nora had heard that I was going into the navy, so she said the meal would be on the house. I ordered the most expensive thing on the menu—stuffed pork chops.

On the morning of doomsday, Dad came into my room at half-past six. "Bill," he said, "I'm going to carry on my usual routine today. I'm going to work.

"I just want to wish you the best. We will all be praying for you. You know what you have been taught here at home, and we expect the best from you."

I said, "Okay, Dad."

He nodded and left.

After breakfast I went upstairs for my bag, and when I came down again Mother said, "Bill, I'm not even going out on the porch to say good-bye to you. You leave just like you're going to school. I think that will be easiest for both of us."

"Yes," I said. "Let's do it that way."

She held up a book. "I bought this Bible for you, Bill. I want you to keep it with you all the time. And I want you to read it."

I took it from her. "I'll read it." Then I did something I

had never done before. I kissed my mother. "Good-bye," I said.

"I'll see you later, Bill."

At the post office were three other boys heading for Pittsburgh, and only one boy's parents had come down to see him off. I didn't envy him the chore of saying good-bye to his folks in public. We were given our train tickets and the four of us went over to the railroad station for the 9:45 train. I got a surprise. At the station were a bunch of kids from school who had cut class to come down and see me off. Among them were Martha Sanders and Louie Morgan. The crowd kept me too busy to think about what was happening, and it wasn't until I was on the train and had a vision of my crumpled body lying on a battlefield that I began to cry. Then I realized that I was in the navy and wouldn't see any battlefields, so I cut it out.

In Pittsburgh I was formally sworn in, then given another physical. For two days, then, we all took a battery of written examinations. We were told to specify what kind of duty we wanted. In view of the fact that I wanted to become an auto mechanic someday, I put down motor machinist training. The second evening, thirty-four prospective machinists were called out and an ensign said, "Men, you're to report to the base at Bainbridge, Maryland. Which one is William Bair?" Startled, I said that I was. "You're in charge." He handed me a thick envelope containing our papers. I wondered what traits of leadership I had displayed to make me a commanding officer on my second day in the navy, then glancing at the list of names on the envelope I saw that mine was first alphabetically.

After the overnight train trip we were taken to the base

by bus, where we were given breakfast: powdered milk, powdered eggs, baked beans, and fried potatoes. The combination turned into cement as we swallowed it. Because we had traveled all night, we were given the day off so that we could get some sleep. I slept for seven hours without rolling over once. Then somebody came roaring into the barracks hollering that if we wanted any supper we'd better get over to the mess hall in a hurry. On the menu was something called Spanish rice: boiled rice and stewed tomatoes. Ten minutes after I ate it, it came back up. I spent the next three days in sick bay, vomiting.

After three months in boot camp I was assigned to an ORU barracks. At 3:00 A.M. my first night there, the light clicked on and a chief came down the aisle, hitting bunks with his fist and counting up to seven. My bunk was number five. Then he announced: "You seven men have just been transferred from machinist school to cooks-and-bakers school, and they want you over there right away. Let's go!"

So that's how I became a cook in the navy. I didn't mind it much. In fact, it was interesting. My mother had always made cooking seem so simple that I was surprised to find out how much there really was to it.

Mother and Dad started visiting me every Sunday in Bainbridge. Sometimes they brought Martha Sanders along. My father seemed very proud of me, although I couldn't understand why. And I could tell that my mother was glad I was going to become a cook—no matter how heavy the combat, surely nobody was going to let the cook get hurt. On my first leave, I bought Martha an engagement ring. It cost seventy-nine dollars. Neither her family nor mine thought much of the whole idea, since we were both so young and I was to be away so much.

After cooking school I was assigned to an amphibious unit of six hundred men scheduled to go to Scotland for training, then take part in a hush-hush landing in Europe. On the way over, our ship was surrounded by a wolf pack of German submarines. The skipper got orders to head north to the safety of the Greenland coast, while American and British subchasers went after the Germans. We were a scared bunch of men that night. It was the first time I dug out my mother's Bible and read it. I had read the Bible before, of course, in Sunday school, but it never meant much. That night reading the Bible produced a strange sense of comfort.

We trained in Scotland for about six months. By then, I was becoming a seasoned sailor. I tried hard liquor but didn't care much for it. I enjoyed beer, and I became a heavy smoker. Pub crawling with my friends was almost a nightly event. Although we were engaged, Martha Sanders and I had agreed that we would date other people occasionally while we were apart, as long as nothing serious developed. My favorite evenings were when a girl would take me home to have supper with her folks. That's what I missed most in the navy—being part of a family.

Then my outfit got its travel orders, and we all knew what that meant: a beach landing somewhere on the coast of Europe. At the last minute, six men were held back and assigned to maintain our old base. I was one of them. At first I was outraged. My buddies were going into combat and I wanted to be with them. A few weeks later, news came that most of my unit had been wiped out in the invasion landing. I was stunned. I dug out my mother's Bible again, but I couldn't bring myself to read it. I just sat there, holding the Bible in my hands, and thinking, Why me, God? Why should You save me? Maybe You have something for me to do. Maybe someday You'll tell me. Meanwhile most of my buddies are with You right now, so just—take care of them. I sat there a long time, thinking such thoughts, wondering why me, of all people.

A few months after that, I was transferred to the south of England, where I cooked for a group of construction workers who were building a navy hospital. When I finally got to Europe, it wasn't with the navy but with the army. For some reason, the army ran short of cooks, so a number of navy cooks were assigned to help out. I landed in Belgium with the Twenty-ninth Division of the Ninth Army. We worked our way through Holland to Bremerhaven, where we helped clean wreckage out of the harbor so our ships could use it. Then we moved inland. I was setting up an outdoor kitchen in a cornfield when I was told that Germany had surrendered.

Reversing the traffic of men and supplies took a few months, during which I cooked for the officers of headquarters company. I got back to England at last, only to discover there was a two-month wait for ships to the States. But the next day I learned that an army tanker had bunks for five cooks who would be willing to work their way across the Atlantic. I volunteered.

The first thing I did when I got to New York was call home. I'll never forget hearing my mother's voice again, after two years. I was given a thirty-day leave and took the first train home. Mother met the train, running to me when she saw me, and I kissed her for the second time in my life. My youngest sister was with her. So was Martha Sanders. The month passed quickly while Martha and I made plans for our future. I spent the rest of the war aboard the *Macon,* a heavy-duty cruiser assigned to the Caribbean Sea.

When I got home, Martha Sanders told me she had been dating a young man named Frank Lewis and they were discussing marriage. Frank Lewis turned out to be a combination of a movie star and an ace halfback, and I knew I was in trouble. The real difficulty was religion. Martha was a devout Christian; so was Frank, and this gave him a head start on me with Martha, regardless of everything else he had going for him. I gave them my blessing, whatever that was worth at the time. They got married. We are all still good friends.

With my navy experience in baking and cooking, I went to work in Aunt Nora's Cake Shop and Tearoom for the time being. As baking was a specialty there, it was easy for me to manage the baking of such mouth-watering goodies as homemade cookies, rolls, pies, layer cakes, and doughnuts.

Evenings, I went to night school so that I could work toward my high-school diploma. One of my subjects was woodshop. One night I had some oak boards to cut down. I put three of the boards up to the electric saw and started pressing. But I had failed to adjust the blade properly. Suddenly the boards cracked and went flying. The momentum carried me forward, causing my left hand to strike the blades. Next thing I knew, I had cut off a couple of fingers.

I couldn't believe my eyes. I said to a boy near me, "Hey, I think I cut off my fingers."

He said, "Yeah?" Then he looked. "My God, you did!"

I ran to the teacher. "Mr. Lance, I think I've cut my fingers off." I still couldn't believe it.

He said, "Let's see." I showed him. "My God, you have!" He got some cotton from a cabinet and wrapped my hand in it, then rushed me to the hospital.

My mother was as angry as she was distressed. She said, "God must have something important for you to do with your life, Bill Bair. Otherwise, nobody as stupid as you would survive."

# 4

I wanted to meet girls. I asked a friend if he could line me up with a date; a few days later he told me that a group of his friends were throwing a moonlight swimming party and that there would be a girl in need of an escort. That's how I met Marilyn Love. The night of the party, I drove out to her house to pick her up. Instead of just coming out after she answered the door she had me go in and meet her whole family. That seemed nice. Marilyn was nice, too. She was very pretty.

On the way to the party, I lit up a cigarette. Marilyn asked, "Are you a Christian, Bill?"

"Yes."

She said, "Christians don't smoke."

Oh, oh. One of those. I asked, "Where does the Bible say 'Thou shalt not smoke' ?"

"It doesn't," she said, "but the Bible does say that your body is the temple of the Lord. Smoking is harmful to your body. It's being disrespectful to the temple of the Lord."

I threw the cigarette away, not because she had convinced me, but because I wanted her to change the subject. She changed to: "I suppose you drink, too."

I was getting a little annoyed. I said, "Yes, I drink. And so did Jesus. Jesus drank wine. He even made the stuff."

"That was different," she said. "In those days, wine was considered food, part of the meal."

"That's exactly the way I look at it," I said.

We were silent for a few minutes. Then Marilyn said, "We're not getting off to a good start, are we?"

"I don't know yet," I said. "So far, you've knocked smoking and drinking. What's next?"

She asked, "Where do you work, Bill?"

"I'm a cook at my aunt's restaurant. What do you do?"

"I'm a telephone operator. What did you do during the war?"

So we were off, getting to know each other, and we were in a good mood when we reached the party. We all swam for a while, and then we settled down around a campfire, toasting hot dogs and singing. As Marilyn and I were returning to her home, she said, "Bill, I apologize for nagging you before about your habits."

I said, "You didn't nag. You just expressed your opinions."

I dated Marilyn once or twice a week for about three months, and rare was the evening when Marilyn didn't have to apologize again for bringing up the subjects of my smoking and drinking. Sometimes we'd pass a bar where I knew some of my friends would be. Marilyn would wait in the car while I went in for a couple of beers. This always made me feel ridiculous, but neither of us would budge an inch from our viewpoints. Occasionally we would double-date with

Marilyn's brother John and his wife Bea. John Love was even more outspoken than Marilyn in his criticism of what he called my filthy habits. I was getting a little fed up with all this, and I came to the conclusion that Marilyn and I were a bad match. I stopped calling her.

But I couldn't stop thinking about her. Another three months passed. One day I went hunting and got a four-point deer, and as I was butchering it in the restaurant I thought it would be a nice gesture to take a roast over to the Love family. Mrs. Love was delighted with the roast, and Marilyn and I started seeing each other again.

The Loves were Methodists. Mostly out of habit, I continued to attend the Salem Reformed Church on Sundays with my parents. As the months passed, Marilyn started inviting me to go to church with her. It didn't make any difference to me where I went—to me, all churches were alike. For Marilyn, there was nothing but Methodism.

The first Sunday I went to her church, the minister zeroed in on the evils of tobacco and alcohol. I was sure Marilyn had put him up to it. But I went a few more times with her, and every Sunday it was the same. I came to the conclusion that smoking and drinking were the only sins Methodists knew about.

I had worked in Aunt Nora's restaurant about two years when her husband suddenly died. Grief stricken, she wanted to get away on a long trip. She offered to sell the restaurant to me, but I realized that I still knew next to nothing about the business end, and I didn't want to risk ruining the place with bad management. Other people bought the restaurant and, after a year and a half, decided to bring in their own kitchen staff, so I was out of a job.

When I couldn't find anything else in Altoona, I went to Philadelphia to look around. Nothing. On the way back, I stopped off at a pastry shop in York to ask if they needed anybody. They did. I moved into a boardinghouse in York, and went home on weekends. But the longer this went on the less I liked it. The two years I was in Europe hadn't seemed as long as one of these weeks. I hadn't known Marilyn Love then.

I guessed it showed. One weekend when I was home, my brother Allan sized me up and said, "Bill, why don't you move back to Altoona?"

I said, "I'd like to, Allan, but what would I do for a job?"

"You can come to work with the gas company," he said. He worked in the office there.

"Does the gas company need a cook?"

He laughed. "No. You'd have to start as a ditch digger. All new men do."

That didn't bother me. "What does it pay?"

"A dollar and a quarter an hour."

I shook my head. "I'm making $2.10 an hour now."

"But think of what you're paying in York for room and board," Allan said. "Think of the gas, coming home weekends. It would just about even out."

I said I'd think about it. That evening, I asked Marilyn, "Do you think you could be happy married to a ditch digger?"

"I wouldn't care what kind of work my husband did," she said, "just so he'd be a good Christian."

"Who didn't smoke or drink?"

"Right."

"You sure make it rough on a guy."

The following week, I took a bunch of examinations at the gas company in Altoona, and was hired as a ditch digger. I found that I liked it. Working outdoors was much more enjoyable than working in a stifling kitchen. The physical exertion put some muscles where baby fat had lingered. I felt better. At the end of the day, instead of scraping flour from under my fingernails I scraped good Pennsylvania soil. And I was very happy to be home.

By now, Marilyn and I knew we were going to get married someday. And we both knew exactly what we would be getting. I would be getting a religious fanatic and she would be getting a hopeless sinner.

And then that summer I had the accident which meant she would be getting an invalid as well. About forty-five miles from town was a quarry that had become a popular swimming hole. There was no diving board at the place, just a forked tree at the water's edge; we'd climb up four or five feet to where the trunk separated and dive from there. You had to give yourself a good outward spring because under the water, just below the tree, was a big boulder. I had dived off that tree hundreds of times.

This particular Sunday afternoon, Marilyn and I were at a picnic there with a large group of friends and relatives. I was up in the tree when my mother arrived on the far side of the quarry. "Hey, Ma," I hollered, "watch your son, the diving champ!" Somehow I failed to give myself enough spring. I hit the underwater boulder head-on. I blacked out and began to sink. Fortunately, my friends had seen what happened and several of them jumped into the water and hauled me out. On shore, my head was bleeding and hurt badly. I was taken to the nearest doctor, who told me I was going to have a headache from the bump for a few days. But he didn't see any other damage and said he wouldn't even have to use stitches on my torn scalp. He bandaged me up and I did have a headache for a few days. After that I seemed to be all right.

About a month later, I was home one evening, reading the paper in the living room, when I felt in the mood for a cup of coffee. I got up and headed for the kitchen. I had taken a step or two when a sudden dizziness swept over me. There was a ringing in my ears and the next thing I knew I was lying on the floor. I must have been unconscious for about fifteen minutes. When I came to, I had the feeling that I had been crying, and there was a bad taste in my mouth. I opened my eyes and saw a doctor standing over me.

I asked, "What happened?"

He said, "You've had a convulsion."

"How come?"

"Your mother told me about your accident at the quarry. That could have caused it."

"But the doctor said I wasn't hurt that bad."

"It might be more serious than he thought. I want you to see a specialist."

Two days later, my mother and I went to the specialist. A lot of X rays were taken and I was given a series of tests. Two days after that, we were given the bad news. I had suffered minor brain damage. Surgery might help, but the prospects were so minimal that the effort wasn't worth the risk. I would probably continue to experience convulsions for the rest of my life. The doctor told my mother how to treat me if I had an attack at home. He advised me to give up driving, at least until some pattern of the attacks might develop and I would know when to expect them. He prescribed tranquilizers.

It was a terrible thing to have to live with. I wondered what it would do to my relationship with Marilyn. I hadn't told her about the first convulsion, hoping it would never happen again, but knowing now that it would, I realized Marilyn had a right to know that not only would she be marrying a ditch digger, but a ditch digger with something wrong in his head.

On our next date, I pulled up to the side of a country road and told her. I couldn't look at her as I talked. She didn't make any comment for a while, and then she said, "We can live with this, Bill. I'm glad you told me. I'll know what to do now if you have an attack when we're together. It doesn't make any difference, Bill, with us."

No pattern developed for me. I would sometimes go weeks without an attack; other times I'd have attacks two or three days in a row. Fortunately, when I was out of the house, the signals gave me a few moments to get away by myself, and so, outside of my family and a few close friends, nobody knew about my condition for quite some time. But I realized this could not go on forever. One day on the job, I was climbing out of a ditch to go get some piping when the signals struck. There was no place to hide. I managed to walk as far as the pile of pipes. Then I lay prone, pretending to be looking into the pipes to see if they were clean. It didn't work. When I came to, the men were standing over me, studying me. I cleaned my face. I said, "That binge last night must have been wilder than I thought. I guess I'm still hung over." I could tell they didn't believe me.

In spite of this, not long afterwards I got a promotion working on a meter truck, going around town installing meters. I began to feel like a real executive.

Even before our marriage, I'd bought a home. The Salem Reformed Church was selling the old parsonage next door to it; with the aid of a loan from my Dad I made the down payment. As Marilyn and I worked to turn the old house into our dream home, I tried to talk her out of a big church wedding. Wedding pranks, I warned her, were a tradition with my crowd. When Mike and Bernice Briggs got married, for example, they held their reception on the lawn of her aunt's home. Nearby was a muddy river. As Mike was strolling among the guests, showing off in his rented tuxedo, several of us picked him up, carried him to the river, and threw him in.

Bill and Evelyn Foster got married at a Catholic mass one Saturday morning. Breakfast was to be served to everybody afterward, and there was to be a big reception in the evening. After the mass, Bill came over to the gang, expecting to be congratulated. We grabbed him, threw him into a car, and drove him to a hunting lodge about fifty miles out of town that we had stocked with a lot of beer. That evening, when we delivered Bill to the reception, Evelyn's father was going to have us all arrested—until somebody remembered that I had baked the three-tier wedding cake and if I wasn't at the party it wouldn't be either. Marilyn listened to a few more of these stories and agreed to elope.

The secret date was April 19, 1952. Mack Brubaker and Sally Valentine went with us as best man and maid of honor. It was a beautiful spring day; the apple blossoms were already out. We made the trip to Winchester, West Virginia, where there was no mandatory waiting period, in my Oldsmobile 88 convertible. The four of us felt very sly and very happy, certain that no one else knew what we were doing. In Winchester we asked a postman, "Do you know where we can get married around here?"

"Yes," he said. "Mr. Smucker. The Reverend Smucker. Go down two blocks and turn to the left and he's the second house." The Reverend Smucker was a very old man. He looked like an underweight Santa Claus, and had a Pennsylvania-Dutch accent we could scarcely understand. After filling out a couple of short forms, Marilyn and I found ourselves standing in front of the fireplace in his living room. He told us that we were the 1,264th couple he had married right in that spot. The ceremony began. I looked at Marilyn. She was wearing a dark blue suit, blue hat, and veil to match. She was beautiful. I hoped she wasn't regretting that we weren't in a church. I hoped she didn't feel that our vows would mean less because of this.

For reasons which Mr. Smucker was unable to make clear to us, he had to marry us a second time but in another county. We followed him in his car across the county line to what looked like an outdoor chapel—an altar surrounded by flowers. It was very pretty and churchy, and Marilyn and I were married a second time. Before leaving us, Mr. Smucker gave me a few of his cards for any of my eloping friends.

Then Mack Brubaker treated the bridal party to a steak dinner, after which we drove back to Altoona. We dropped Mack and Sally off, and Marilyn and I headed to our home as husband and wife. As we pulled up to the house, the first thing we noticed was the bed hanging out the bedroom window. We found the mattress on the roof of the porch. All the furniture on the first floor was piled in the living room. Every drawer in the house had been emptied; everything in the kitchen cabinets was on the back porch.

Marilyn was so angry she just stood in the middle of the mess and cried. It took about four hours to put the house into some semblance of order. Then, around three in the morning, we heard footsteps on the stairs. Into the bedroom came the gang, six or seven fellows with their girl friends, all carrying candles. They stood around the bed singing lullabies, and wouldn't leave until we got up and made them some coffee.

When they finally took off, I wouldn't have been surprised if Marilyn had packed up too, and gone home to her mother. Instead, she fixed me with an icy eye.

"I don't know what marriage to you is going to be like," she said, "but I can see already that it isn't going to be dull."

# 5

Marilyn and I had been married a year when John and Bea Love took in Charles, the foster child I'd been so opposed to at first. Marilyn and I were eager to get our own family going, but the months kept passing. Our second year of marriage ended, and Marilyn decided she'd better have a medical examination. The doctor discovered that Marilyn needed some minor corrective surgery, and she went into the hospital for a couple of days. Later he called us to his office. The results of the operation were disappointing: in all likelihood, Marilyn would never bear children. Things were pretty sad around our house for a while.

Then Marilyn suggested that we adopt a baby. I was all for it, but when we checked into it, we learned that so many couples wanted babies we couldn't even get on the waiting list for a long while.

One day Marilyn asked, "Bill, why don't we take a foster child into our home, like Charles?"

I thought about it. "I guess that's the only thing left. Do you think we could get a baby?"

"We can ask. I'd prefer a baby, too," Marilyn said. "But there's one thing we should consider."

"What's that?"

"Suppose we got a baby whose parents were having some temporary trouble. We would have the baby for a while and learn to love him. Then his parents might straighten things out. Where would we be?"

"In worse shape than we are now. But let's look into it. Let's talk to John and Bea."

I expected John Love to give me the horselaugh when he found out that I was about to do exactly what I had reproached him for. Instead, he was delighted. He kept shaking my hand and congratulating me, as though we'd just announced that Marilyn was pregnant. Then he gave us instructions on how to proceed.

Next day, Marilyn called the child welfare office. She was told that a woman would come out to interview us. So that I could be there, an appointment was made for late one weekday afternoon. Marilyn had the house spotless. After I cleaned myself up, she made me show her my fingernails. Then she said, "Bill, don't ruin things by lighting a cigarette while this woman is here." To play it safe, we put away all the ashtrays. When the woman rang the doorbell, we literally jumped.

She turned out to be a very nice person. We chatted in the living room for a while, and then Marilyn suggested we go out on the back porch for coffee. As we went through the house, I caught the woman checking out Marilyn as a housekeeper. You could have eaten off the floor. As we were visiting on the porch, some friends came by and joined us. Fortunately, they were Marilyn's friends, not mine, so nobody asked for a beer. When Marilyn disclosed that she was John Love's sister, the woman beamed, and I was sure we were in. As she left, she said, "There will be a child in this home very soon." That was a happy evening for Marilyn and me.

When I came home from work one afternoon a few days later, I could see that something was on Marilyn's mind. As we sat down on the porch with our coffee, I saw an ashtray on the table. I wouldn't have been surprised if Marilyn had offered me a beer—she was being that eager to please. I waited, all love and suspicion. We talked about unimportant things. Finally Marilyn said offhandedly, "The woman from child welfare called today."

I asked, "Does she have somebody for us?"

"She has two," Marilyn said.

"We have a choice?"

"No. She wants us to take them both."

I dropped my cigarette. "Two kids at once?"

"Yes. They're brother and sister. The woman from child welfare feels they shouldn't be separated."

"I suppose she's right," I said, "but we're in no position to take two kids at once."

"Aren't we?"

I looked at her. "Are we?"

"I don't see why not."

"But it'll be a lot of work for you," I pointed out.

"I won't mind."

I shrugged. "Then it's up to you."

"No, it isn't," Marilyn said. "It's up to you. You're the head of the household. Suddenly having two small children in the house is going to change our lives a great deal. But we'll have something new to live for, something important and beautiful. I want you to want these two children as much as I do."

I suggested, "Could we take them on a trial basis for a while?"

Marilyn shook her head. "I wouldn't do that to a child. We wouldn't do that with our own, would we? When they get here, I want them to know that they're staying here. It would be awful for them to think that they're being tested."

"How old are they?"

"The boy is six and the girl is three."

A boy. I liked that. "When can we get them?"

"I don't know. I didn't give her an answer. I wanted to wait and see how you felt."

I thought about it. "Okay, Mama. Call up the woman at welfare tomorrow and tell her we'll take the two kids and do our best with them."

Marilyn kissed me. "Thanks, Papa." As she headed inside to the kitchen she took the ashtray with her. So the party was over.

The boy's name was Theodore, the girl's Marlene, their nicknames Ted and Marty. They were to be brought to us at four in the afternoon two days later. I took the afternoon off. Marilyn and I wandered around the house, nervous, quiet, unsure. At four, we were together on the back-porch swing, putting away our third gallon of coffee. I asked Marilyn, "Are you sure that woman said four?"

"She said four."

"It's ten after."

"They'll be here." She reached for her coffee, and her hand shook so much she almost dropped the cup.

Finally a station wagon pulled up in the driveway. Marilyn and I were so nervous that neither of us thought of going to the car and being helpful. We just sat there. We watched the woman remove a tricycle from the car, then a toy fire engine, then a shopping bag containing clothes. We found out later that the kids had stolen both the bike and the fire engine from neighbors. A boy and a girl got out of the car. They looked so small, so frail, so frightened, so unbelievably dirty. They were both blondes, but dirt made their hair gray. They badly needed baths and their clothes needed laundering. It wasn't until they had all reached the bottom of the steps that I thought of getting up and saying, "Here, let me help you." By then they were on the porch.

The woman said, "Marlene, Theodore, these are the nice people I was telling you about. You're going to live with them for a while."

The kids didn't look at us. Without a word Marilyn dropped to her knees and took Marlene into her arms. I stepped to the boy and extended my right hand. "Hi, Ted. Welcome to your new home." He ignored me.

The woman said, "Theodore, shake hands with the man and tell him you're glad to be here."

Still without looking at me, Ted took my hand and said, "I'm glad to be here."

"What's wrong with his voice?" I asked, alarmed.

"It's adenoids," the woman said. "In a few weeks, welfare will arrange to have them removed."

I drew her aside where we wouldn't be overheard. "Is anything else wrong with him?"

"He can't tell colors."

"What do you mean?"

"He doesn't know one color from another."

"Is he color-blind?"

"No. He's never been taught the names of colors."

"Well, we can take care of that. Anything else?"

"No."

"What about the girl?"

"She's all right." The woman hesitated, then: "There is one thing, though."

I braced myself. "What?"

"They both cry a lot."

I was relieved. "They'll get over that once they get used to us."

"I suppose so," she said. "Both of them usually cry at the same time, by the way."

"That's natural."

"It can get on your nerves," the woman said, her tone full of experience.

Marilyn released Marlene from the embrace, moved to Ted, and kissed his grimy cheek. She turned to the woman. "Do you have time for a cup of coffee?"

She looked at her watch. "I guess so."

The pot of hot coffee was already on the porch table. Marilyn said, "You take cream, don't you?"

"Yes."

Marilyn took a step toward the door, but I touched her arm. "Ted," I said, "will you please go into the kitchen and get the yellow pitcher that's on the table?"

The woman said, "He won't know which is the yellow one."

I replied, "We've only got one, and it's yellow, so today he learns yellow. Get the yellow cream pitcher, Ted." He hesitated a moment, then headed for the door. As he went through, his hand lingered on the jamb, and the screen door swung shut on it. He howled. I took a few quick steps toward him, when I was stopped by howls from Marty. I didn't know who to go to first. I chose Ted; Marilyn went to Marty. It hadn't been a bad blow, but from the noise coming out of Ted, you would think every bone in his hand was pulverized. I rubbed his hand. "It'll be all right in a moment, son. Now get the yellow creamer off the table."

He simmered down a bit and went to the table. Unable to reach the creamer from the floor, he climbed onto a chair. As he wiggled off again, the creamer slipped from his hands and crashed to bits on the floor. More howling. Renewed howls from Marty on the porch. As I cleaned up the mess, I tried to console Ted, telling him it had been an accident that could have happened to anyone. I went back to the porch. "We now don't have a cream pitcher of any color," I told Marilyn. At that moment, Marty, on her bike, rode too close to the edge of the porch and one rear wheel went over. There was no chance of her going over the side, but she evidently thought so. Howls. Howls from Ted.

The welfare woman stood up. "It's getting late. I'd better go. Call me if you need me." And she was down the stairs, across the lawn, into her car, and out of sight in seconds.

Suddenly being alone with the two bewildering children was like baby-sitting for a couple of young tigers. They were into everything, on the porch, in the yard, out on the sidewalk, and every few minutes there would be the yowls. It took me a while to realize that the reason the kids screamed

at every unexpected event was that they expected to be punished. They certainly weren't doing anything that required
punishment. They were in a strange place, with many sur-
prises—they even howled at grasshoppers—so Marilyn and I
were kept busy for a couple of hours, dashing to them, calm-
ing, comforting, explaining.

It began to grow dark. We took the kids inside. Marty
insisted on taking in her bike; Ted wanted his fire engine.
To save the furniture, we confined them both to the kitchen,
while Marilyn started supper. We had to shout to be heard
over the rumble of the fire engine on the linoleum. As Marty
kept circling the room, she bumped into things repeatedly,
and on every third trip ran over my foot. I finally had
enough. I lifted her off the bike and put it on the back porch.
Shrieks. Shrieks from Ted. To give Ted something of his
own to scream about, I put his fire engine on the porch too.
The commotion was deafening.

I forget what Marilyn served that night, but Marty and
Ted both said they didn't like it and wouldn't eat it. I had
never studied child psychology, but it seemed to me that
the kids were refusing to eat to let us know that they weren't
as yet buying this new setup they found themselves in. For
ten or fifteen minutes, Marilyn and I pretended to enjoy our
dinner, chatting, trying to bring the kids into the conversation. I began to feel a little concerned. I asked Marilyn with
my eyes if we should give in and fix them something they
would eat. Marilyn shook her head. Another ten or fifteen
minutes passed, then Marilyn asked, "Bill, would you like
some more of anything?"

I said, "No thanks, honey. I've had plenty. It was deli-
cious!"

"All right, then," Marilyn said, "I'll start clearing away the dishes." She picked up her plate and reached for Ted's.

Ted sat up and pointed to a corner of his plate. "What's that?"

"That's squash," Marilyn said.

"Is it any good?"

"Oh, yes. Yummy."

"I never had it," Ted said. He picked up his fork and sampled, then reluctantly began to nibble at the rest of his food. Without a word, Marty picked up her spoon. Neither of them ate much—they still refused a complete surrender—but at least neither of them would die from starvation during the night.

It hadn't occurred to Marilyn or me to buy any toys and games for the children, assuming, I suppose, that they would bring things of their own. But they brought only the bike and fire engine, both now confined to the outdoors. We wondered what to do with them for the evening. Then Marilyn remembered that in the church next door were some old leaflets of Bible stories for children. I went and got some. Marty and Ted curled up in a big chair with Marilyn and she read to them, explaining the illustrations.

Around eight, Marilyn announced, "Well, children, it's getting near bedtime. Come on, I'll give you your baths now." Marty followed willingly enough, but Ted stood his ground. Marilyn called, "Ted?"

Ted said, "I want my dad to wash me."

Marilyn said, "Your father isn't here, Ted, so I'll wash you."

Ted didn't move. He said, "I want my dad to wash me."

I said, "Ted, don't be silly. We can't expect your father to come way over here just to give you a bath."

He glared at me, clearly exasperated. "I don't mean my father. I mean my dad," he said. "I mean you."

I looked at him a long time. Then I looked at Marilyn. She was beaming. She said, "Bill, I think he's just hooked you."

I looked at Ted again. I said, "Yeah. It feels good. You two go ahead. I'll give my son his bath later."

When they were both cleaned up and tucked in their beds, Marilyn asked me to say the good-night prayer. I don't remember what I said, but I do know that I thanked God for sending us these two beautiful kids. I was hooked on both of them.

Although the welfare department allotted us one dollar a day for each child, I soon found out that you cannot raise a kid on that kind of money. Marty and Ted had come to us with practically nothing, and there was so much they needed. The time came when I realized that in order to provide I had to earn more. I told Marilyn one night that I was going to do a little moonlighting a few nights a week. The only night job I could find was working with a friend converting furnaces from coal to gas. It was a rotten job. The furnace had to be thoroughly cleaned before it could be converted, which meant crawling inside the thing with a load of rags. Within a few weeks, my hands were permanently laced with soot. The money was good, but I earned every penny of it. I knew there had to be an easier way.

The easier way came along by chance—or at least that was the way I viewed it at the time. A salesman came to our home one evening and described a frozen-food plan that included a freezer thrown in at a good price. An assortment of frozen foods would be delivered to the house each week, and we would pay for food and appliance together on the installment plan. I liked the whole idea. I liked it so much, in fact, that I kept asking the salesman questions. He said it was something new that was catching on fast all over the country; in fact, his district manager was looking for more salesmen. The next day, I called on this man. Although I had no experience in selling, I was excited about this project and convinced I could get other people excited. The district manager was willing to give me a chance. That evening, I studied all the literature on the service. The next evening after supper I took a walk through the neighborhood and sold the plan to three families. I knew I had found something good. What I didn't know was that I had found something that would change my whole life.

Meanwhile, Marilyn and I had almost forgotten that Marty and Ted were not our own children. We loved them so much and responded so naturally to their "Daddy" and "Mommy" that the fact slipped our minds that they were with us on a day-to-day basis. They had been taken out of their home; but they could be sent back whenever the courts saw fit to send them. The truth was brought home to us bluntly one Saturday afternoon when the children had been with us about four months. I had taken them with me to the local supermarket, Marty in the shopping cart, Ted helping me push it.

Suddenly Ted cried, "Aunt Edna! Aunt Edna! Marty, there's Aunt Edna!" He went running pell-mell to an attractive, middle-aged woman I had never seen before. Ted dragged her over to Marty, and they were all hugging and kissing each other and crying. That's when I remembered that Marty and Ted had had another life before they became part of mine. I already knew there were other children in the family—Judy, age two, and a boy about a year old. Judy and the little boy were also in foster homes. The welfare department had a policy of not letting families know where their children had been placed, but now as I saw how happy Marty and Ted were to see their aunt, I wondered if this was really a good idea. I felt that the victims of an unfortunate home situation need not necessarily be turned into strangers to each other. A child, I felt, had the right to know that not only was he loved by his foster family but that he had a natural family with which he shared loves and loyalties. Aunt Edna told me that she'd had no idea where the children were. She lived miles away, just happened to be in our neighborhood, and had decided to do some shopping on an impulse. I told her where we lived and invited her to visit the children whenever she wished.

When we got home, Marty and Ted were all excited as they told Marilyn about Aunt Edna. I watched Marilyn's face. She was smiling and saying how nice it was, but I could read her thoughts—they were the same as mine: we would have to share the children. That night, after the children went to bed, we talked about it. There wasn't much to discuss; we both felt the same way. The following day, Marilyn telephoned the social worker at child welfare and told her that we wanted Marty and Ted to have regular visits with their sister and brother when he was old enough, and with their parents. The woman was surprised. She said most foster parents didn't feel this way but, since we did, she was sure something could be arranged.

These reunions were always a lot of fun. I especially liked Judy. The first time she came to our home, I happened to be holding Marty on my knee. Judy came right over and climbed onto my other knee, kissed Marty, and then kissed me and put an arm around my neck. I was hooked again.

If we had any doubts about the wisdom of what we were doing, Ted's and Marty's reaction convinced us. They enjoyed seeing their parents. They loved their parents. Without requiring any explanation they seemed to understand that they could not live together as a family for the present time. And they were happy with the situation as it was. Over the years, I was to see this attitude in children confirmed many times. No matter how dreadful the home situation was, the child still loved his parents, was ready to accept their weaknesses and forgive them again and again, and, with surprising maturity, adjust happily to other living circumstances.

Marilyn and I were approaching our fourth wedding anniversary. One night after the kids went to bed, I was finishing the paper when I caught Marilyn's eyes on me. "Bill, I have some news for you."

I laid down the paper. "Yes?"

"I'm pregnant."

# 6

As the months passed, all Marty and Ted wanted to talk about was the new baby who was coming to join the family. They didn't care whether it would be a little brother or a little sister. Neither did Marilyn and I.

With my family growing, I spent more evenings out, selling the food plan. One month, I sold it to thirty-two families and earned close to twelve hundred dollars in commissions, as well as a free trip to Milwaukee for Marilyn and me to visit the company's processing plant.

As Marilyn's time drew near, I became a nervous wreck. I was installing gas meters all this time, and my truck was linked to the office by radio. I had arranged with the office for Marilyn to call me there, her message to be radioed to me wherever I was working. During the last few weeks of Marilyn's pregnancy, I virtually flew back to the truck whenever I heard our signal.

It was four o'clock one afternoon when the radio message came. Marilyn had gone to the hospital around three; a friend had taken Ted and Marty to her mother's. I picked up my car at the plant, drove straight to the hospital, and insisted on seeing Marilyn. I'd been with her only a few minutes when the doctor came in. "Get out of here, Bill Bair," he said. "Those filthy work clothes of yours are contaminating this entire ward. We've got plenty of time. Go home. Change clothes. Eat something. This may take all night."

I went home and changed, but I knew I could not eat anything. Heading back to the hospital, I bought two boxes of cigars and spent the evening passing them out to people I didn't know. Every time a doctor came out of the maternity ward, I'd jump at him, but it was never our doctor, so I would just give the startled man a cigar. It was 11:45 before our doctor came out, grinning. He said, "It's a girl. Six pounds. Mother and daughter in fine shape." I gave him the last cigar.

We had agreed if it was a girl to call her Jeanne. I was allowed to see Marilyn briefly, and the first word we both uttered was "Jeanne." We were very happy.

I got down to the newsstand just in time to buy the operator's last box of cigars. I opened it and gave him one and told him about my daughter Jeanne. He started to tell me about his kids—all twelve of them—but I had other plans. I went to the tavern where my friends hung out, and this was one night I didn't have to pay for a single beer. I don't remember how many beers I downed, but I do remember it was around two when I got home. Only then did I realize I had not told the family about Jeanne. I spent the next two hours on the phone. Nobody minded being awakened in the middle of the night to hear the good news, and they attributed my giddiness to my joy.

A couple of months after Jeanne was born, Dick Kelso, the gas company's personnel representative in Pittsburgh, visited Altoona, and sent word that he wanted to talk to me. I was surprised by his first question.

"Bill, do you like working for the gas company?"

I said, "I like it very much."

"What do you like about it?"

"Oh," I said, considering, "I like keeping on the move. I like meeting people—talking to them—getting to know them."

He said, "Do you think you'd like selling?"

"I know I would. I've got a side job, Dick. In the evenings, I go around town and sell freezers and a food plan. I've sold a couple of hundred in less than a year."

"Freezers?" he said, his eyes almost falling out of his head. "*Electric* freezers?"

It was the first time it occurred to me that I'd been selling for the competition.

"Bill," he said, "how would you like to go into sales for the gas company? You'd be working mostly with stores and architects and building contractors. It would be public relations as well as selling."

I thought a minute. "The company already has men around here doing that."

"It wouldn't be around here," he said. "It would be in the Pittsburgh area. The company needs salesmen around Pittsburgh."

"Would I have to move there?"

"Probably. Would you consider that?"

"I don't know. I'd have to talk it over with my wife."

"Think about it," he said. "I'll get back to you in a couple of weeks."

Marilyn and I didn't know what to make of it. Certainly it was a great opportunity for me. But—what about my limitations? I hadn't finished high school. I had no mind for statistics. It was easy enough for me to talk to strangers; but if they had much reverence for the English language, I knew my grammar made them wince. I was pretty sure I could get along with store operators and maybe even building contractors, but I'd be out of my depth for certain with architects. And what about the convulsions that were still occurring as unpredictably as ever?

Two weeks later, when I got back to the plant at the end of the day, there was a message from Kelso, telling me to be at the main office in Pittsburgh at ten o'clock the next morning. For me, this was like an order to show up at the White House. I wasn't sure what to wear. I had always preferred flashy clothes and owned a blinding wardrobe, but I thought this occasion called for something more subdued. That morning, I put on the black suit I wore only to funerals. Marilyn stared at me as I came downstairs. "Do you intend to wear black for the rest of your life? Be yourself, Bill." I switched to a white sport coat and blue slacks. We left the children with the Loves so Marilyn could go with me to Pittsburgh. She waited in the lobby of the company headquarters as I went up to the ninth floor for my appointment with Mr. McWilliams, the Assistant General Sales Manager. I was scared to death.

McWilliams turned out to be a very pleasant man, friendly and outgoing. One of the first things he said to me was, "I like your jacket, Bill." He told me we would be having our talk in the conference room, with Mr. Yost, General Sales Manager, and Dick Kelso. When we reached the big wood-paneled room, the others were already there. For more than two hours, the three of them questioned me. I told them about the diving accident and about my lack of education. They seemed more interested in how I felt about people, how I felt about selling, how I felt about the company. I didn't expect them to discuss me in front of myself, but finally McWilliams said to Yost, "What do you think?"

Yost said, "I think we ought to grab him right away."

McWilliams said to Kelso, "Call up Altoona and ask them how soon they can replace Bill."

As Kelso made the call, McWilliams told me that I'd be getting a raise right away of seventy-five dollars a month, which was terrific, and that I would be working in the Western Division. Kelso finished his call and announced, "Altoona can let Bill go in about two weeks."

McWilliams asked me, "Can you move your family here in two weeks?"

"I don't know," I said doubtfully, thinking of the kids, taking Ted out of school, leaving our families. "But I can be here in two weeks myself. I have a sister living here; I can stay with her."

"Work it out any way you want," McWilliams said. "There's a training course starting in two weeks, and I want you to attend it."

"I'll be there."

Marilyn and I agreed to give this new development in our lives a six-month trial. That would be time enough to find out if I really liked my new job and was any good at it before we uprooted the kids and sold the house.

Meanwhile, I would be a weekend husband and father. My sister Elda was living in Pittsburgh. I moved most of my clothes to her house and reported to the company's facilities at Turtle Creek to begin my training. There were about twenty men in the group, and we spent the days attending classes at which we learned about the company's appliances and services, its policies, and the selling techniques that were preferred. Monday of the second week the instructor said, "Gentlemen, we will have just two more days of lectures and demonstrations. Wednesday, Thursday, and Friday will be given over to tests."

I felt sick. School again. I worried all day. That evening I called Marilyn and asked her to put in a few good words with the Lord for me about the tests. She said, "I will, Bill. And remember that you can pray for yourself, too. If the Lord wants you to get that job, He'll handle the tests."

He did. Wednesday morning when I arrived at Turtle Creek, there was a message for me to call a Mr. Wes Cullen, sales supervisor of the company's Western Division. When the operator put me through he said, "I understand you've had experience fixing boilers."

"No, sir," I said, wondering where he'd gotten such an idea. "I once had experience with furnaces, converting from coal to gas."

"Oh. Well, do you know anything about boilers?"

"I've never worked on one, but I'm a pretty good mechanic."

"Let me tell you my problem," he said. "I've got a good customer over in Gibsonia who bought a boiler from us some time back, and has been having trouble with it. Today he can't get it to work at all. Can you come up here to Glenshaw? We'll drive over to Gibsonia and you can see what you can do."

I said, "Mr. Cullen, I just finished the training course and I'm facing a lot of tests today."

"This is more important. You head up here right away, okay?"

I drove to Glenshaw and met Wes Cullen. We went over to Gibsonia, and we were able to fix the boiler. Back at Glenshaw, Cullen asked, "Have they told you yet where you'll be assigned?"

I said, "A couple of weeks ago, Mr. McWilliams told me Aliquippa."

"Aliquippa? That's my district," Cullen said. "Listen, Bill, come back here tomorrow and let's spend the day together. I want to get to know you better. Friday we can go to Aliquippa and I'll introduce you to some of our customers."

"But what about the tests?"

"Forget about the tests," he said. "I'll talk to McWilliams. Bill, I watched you work today. Not only did you fix the boiler, but you won that man over for life. I'll see you tomorrow."

I was a very happy man as I drove back to Pittsburgh, and all I could think of to say was, "Lord, You really did it!"

Although I had been instructed in company sales techniques, I soon found myself developing a pattern of my own, a pattern which reflected the advice Marilyn so often gave me: "Be yourself." I met salesmen from other firms and their approach seemed to be to make as many calls as possible every day and don't waste any time batting the breeze. But batting the breeze had been a lifelong pleasure of mine. I wanted to be more than a salesman: I wanted to be a friend. Many times I clerked in a store all day when I learned that the owner was short of help. I enjoyed decorating windows— and it gave me a chance to put the gas appliances up front. About once a week, I'd arrive at a customer's store loaded down with hamburger meat, buns, and all the trimmings, and spend the day grilling hamburgers for the store's customers, giving them a little pitch about the grill itself and the advantages of using gas.

Whenever I learned that a church or a school or a club was going to have some special function, I was there, helping out. Wes Cullen got the idea of having Aunt Jemima, the pancake lady, make a personal appearance in Aliquippa. All the schools, churches, and clubs got behind the pancake festival. We had a big parade, with three school bands. With proportions that reminded me of cooking for the navy, I made a huge oval pancake, five-by-three feet, and we exhibited it in the office. The Catholic church let us use an auditorium where we set up a battery of stoves (gas, of course) and made all the pancakes people could eat. It was that sort of job, something happening all the time, mixing business with pleasure. I loved it. Marilyn and I started looking for a house in Aliquippa.

God seemed to be in the move all the way. When the Salem Reformed Church heard we were leaving, they jumped at the chance to buy back the house; the congregation was growing, they needed a home for a full-time pastor again.

And then the sky of our particular heaven fell in. A letter arrived from the child welfare department. They congratulated us on my promotion; they would start looking at once for a new home for Theodore and Marlene. Not understanding, we called them up. It was a department rule, the voice on the phone explained: foster children could only be placed in the county they came from. We weren't to feel bad; it happened all the time that foster parents were transferred; they already had the name of another suitable family.

I put down the phone and Marilyn and I stared at each other. It had simply never occurred to us that we would not be able to move Ted and Marty. Still not believing it, we went to the child welfare office. We wrote letters. Everyone we knew wrote letters. The answer was always the same. The department could not make an exception for an individual case.

What were we to do now? We no longer had either a job or a house in Altoona. And even if we found another place for Marilyn and the kids to stay, what sort of family would that be for children to grow up in, with the father home only on weekends?

In the middle of a sleepless night Marilyn said suddenly, "Bill, I believe the Lord has known all along that we were going to have to give up Marty and Ted some day."

"What makes you think that?" I asked.

"Jeanne."

"Jeanne?"

"Yes," she said. "As you know, the doctors once told us that I would never be able to bear children. That's why we took Marty and Ted. Well, I believe the Lord knew that we'd have to give them up someday, and that's why He gave us Jeanne."

I shook my head. "I don't know."

About ten days later, Marilyn called me at Elda's with the news that the caseworker had been to see her; the children would be moved to their new home the following Monday. I didn't want Marilyn to go through something like this alone, so I made arrangements to take Monday off. The weekend was miserable. Every time Marilyn or I tried to tell the children what was about to happen, the words caught in our throats and tears filled our eyes. We couldn't say a thing the whole weekend, and on Monday morning the children still had no idea that they were about to move. When the caseworker arrived, I told her the problem.

She said, "I can understand. Are their things packed?"

"No," I said. "We were afraid to do even that, in case they asked questions."

"Send the children to me," she said. "You and Mrs. Bair can do the packing while I talk to them."

I sent the kids to the woman, and Marilyn and I went into their room to pack their clothes and toys. Twenty minutes later, when we entered the living room, Marty and Ted seemed almost excited about making the move. This hurt a little, but I realized they were very young and perhaps didn't understand that they were going away for good. It took three trips for me to carry everything to the station wagon and pack it. Then Marilyn came out with the woman and the children. It was when the kids turned to us to say good-bye that both Marilyn and I broke down. Marilyn clung to the kids, sobbing, and if she had told me that our move to Pittsburgh was off, I would have cheered.

After they left, the house was like a morgue. Marilyn and I couldn't look at each other without choking up. Even little Jeanne seemed to sense that something was wrong, whimpering fretfully in her crib. Lunch was out of the question. The empty chairs at the table would have destroyed us. Finally Marilyn asked, "When are you heading back to Pittsburgh?"

"Right now," I said. "And you and Jeanne are coming with me. Put some things in a bag. What we all need is to get out of this house for a while."

We did not live in that house again more than the few days it took to come back and pack up. That week we decided on a house we had liked in Aliquippa; the gas company paid for the move.

And so we began a new life. I already had many friends in Aliquippa—customers who had become friends, plus people I met through them. Because Marilyn and I both had so many relatives in Altoona, we also went back there at least one weekend a month. When summer came John Love and Lee Harrison, the Methodist pastor, rented cottages on the Jersey seashore, and they invited us to come along. Marilyn and Jeanne did go for a couple of weeks, and I joined them on the weekends.

My last weekend there I arrived to find everyone in a state of excitement. They had met a contractor who was going to put up a string of summer cottages on some property nearby. John and Lee wanted me to join them in buying two adjacent cottages, which we could rent out most of the summer to cover the costs and still have a vacation there ourselves. It sounded like a good investment, so I went along. Now during the long Pennsylvania winter we had a new topic for speculation: would the cottages be ready in time for next summer?

In Aliquippa, Marilyn and I had started attending Shannopin Methodist Church in South Heights. The young couples in our crowd had two things in common: the girls were, like Marilyn, dedicated Christians, and the guys were, like me, not so dedicated. That October, our minister announced that we were going to have a revival. Right away, all the wives talked about attending as many of the meetings as possible and the husbands about ways of getting out of them. The wives had enough time before the first meeting on a Sunday night to line up baby-sitters, so we all went, about ten couples. The theme of the sermon was that a lot of Christians were phonies, pretending to be Christians and leading superficially Christian lives, while all the time holding themselves back, never really surrendering their lives to Christ at all. I didn't like any of this one bit. The preacher was hitting me right between the eyes, making half of me angry, the other half itchy in humiliation. I was glad when we got out of there.

Monday night, only three wives were able to obtain baby-sitters. The others stayed home with the children, but ordered their husbands to the meeting. We all met early at the church, and then walked a couple of blocks to a tavern and had a few beers. As the time of the service neared, Bill Jones said, "Okay, you guys, let's get over there."

I asked, "Bill, are you kidding? We're not going to the meeting."

"You're not? What are you going to tell your wives?"

"That it was a good service with a wonderful message and that we'll baby-sit tomorrow night so they can go."

"But suppose your wife asks you what the message was?"

"They're always the same—phony Christians trying to fool the Lord."

Bill said, "Listen, fellas, maybe I can fool the Lord, but I sure can't fool my wife. If she finds out I didn't attend this meeting, there'll be murder in my house. I'm going."

We all knew we were in the same boat, so we downed the beers and headed for the church. The place was packed. Bill and I managed to find seats together in a pew halfway down the aisle, and the others in the pew behind us. I prepared myself for another itchy sermon.

I was in for a surprise, in more ways than one. The minister began to talk about love. Jesus Christ, he said, was Love personified—Love come alive—and he said we really couldn't love anybody unless we loved people through Him. Human love, he said, was a weak and limited thing, but when we loved people through the Lord, then we could love broadly and importantly, and our lives would mean more to the Lord, to the people we loved, to ourselves. He said we did this by taking the Lord into our lives, by becoming Christians. I thought about this. The person I loved most in my life was Marilyn, and she was a Christian if ever I met one. I realized that if the Lord had blessed our marriage—and I knew He had—it was because of Marilyn, certainly not because of me. I realized, too, that if there was any way I could love Marilyn more, I would do whatever was necessary to achieve it, even if it meant making a public spectacle of myself.

The altar call was made. I heard Bill Jones say, "I'm going up there. That sermon made sense to me."

I grabbed his arm. "Bill, don't be silly. You know what the guys will say."

He said, "I don't care what the guys say. I just care about what the Lord thinks." He got up and went forward.

I knew in my heart that I wanted to go forward, but I

was still the hypocrite. I turned to my friends. "I'm going up there to pray for Bill."

Entering the growing cluster of kneeling people, I located Bill Jones and knelt beside him. He was lost in prayer: a bomb could have exploded in front of him and he wouldn't have noticed. I tried to pray, but no words came to me. Scattered thoughts strayed through my mind. I knew I owed the Lord a lot. He had been good to me countless times, although I had rarely asked Him and never thanked Him. I thanked Him now. But I knew that gratitude wasn't enough. I realized I had to do something. What, though? I thought, Lord, if there's anything You want me to do for You, I wish You'd let me know what it is. I give You my life, if that's worth anything.

I could hear the minister praying. I could hear the kneeling people around me praying. All at once, without warning, something bright as lightning seemed to shine and shiver inside me. I began to feel strangely and incredibly happy.

After the service, I joined my friends outside the church. A couple of them had already taken off—in disgust at what I myself just that night had called exhibitionism. I had picked up several of the guys for the meeting, including Bill Jones, and now I offered to drive them home. Bill said, "No, thanks. I'll walk. I'm feeling too great to sit still in a car." He took off.

The rest of us started home when someone suggested we stop off for a beer. I went along with them. But I found that I didn't have any desire for beer, so I didn't order any. I didn't feel like smoking either. I couldn't stop telling my friends how good I felt. Later, as I dropped the last man off, he said, "Bill, this high you're on is going to last two weeks."

"I'll settle," I said.

When I got home, Marilyn was reading in bed. As I entered the room, I said, "Honey, I feel wonderful!"

Marilyn glanced at me. "Are you drunk, Bill?"

"Yes," I said. "I'm drunk on the Lord."

"You know I don't like you to talk that way."

"It's true," I insisted. "Honey, I'm saved! The Lord saved me tonight. I answered the altar call."

"You went forward?"

"Yes."

"You've always said you'd never do that."

"I know. But tonight I just had to. I just had to go up there."

Marilyn got up and came to me, standing near, studying my face. "Bill, I hope you're serious about this."

"I am serious," I said. "I'm so happy I'm giddy." We found ourselves in an embrace, and I felt as though I was having my first experience with love.

Two weeks later I ran into my doubting friend, and he asked, "Are you still on your high, Bill?"

I laughed. "I don't know what to call it," I said, "but if you mean do I still love the Lord, the answer is yes."

Something else was happening. At first, I didn't pay much attention to it, but as the days passed and then the weeks, and at last two months went by, a wild, incredulous hope began to grow in me. "Marilyn," I said one night in December, "do you realize I haven't had a single convulsion since that night I went forward?"

She nodded. "I've been counting the weeks, too."

"Are you thinking what I'm thinking?"

"I'm thinking we have a very wonderful God."

Christmas was coming, and it seemed to me that Marilyn

was running away with shopping for Jeanne. The house was beginning to look like a department store: toys, books, clothes she wouldn't grow into for years. But when I came upon the erector set—"Honey," I said, "are you sure Jeanne needs all this?"

An uneasy look came over her face. "They aren't all for Jeanne."

"Oh. John and Bea's kids?"

"No. They're for Ted and Marlene."

"Ted and Marty?" I wasn't ready for that. "How can we? We don't even know where they are."

"Oh, Bill," she said, her eyes filling up, "I've got to see them. It's Christmas, Bill. They'll be thinking of us."

"We don't know that," I said. "They're probably perfectly happy where they are. They probably don't even remember us."

"I don't care. I want to see them."

"Don't you think I do—every day that passes? But how could we ever find them? Welfare certainly won't tell us where they are. It's against policy."

"Bill," she pleaded, "please do this for me. We know a lot of people in Altoona. Somebody must know where they are. When we get home for Christmas, telephone your friends, Bill. Find out where they are. Seeing them would be the best present you could give me."

I knew we were not supposed to do this, but Marilyn evidently had her heart set on it, and I just hoped there would be no repercussions. When we got to Altoona just before Christmas, I made a dozen calls before I reached anybody who had any idea where the kids might be. Then I had to make another dozen calls before I tracked them down. I didn't have any trouble identifying myself to the woman who answered the phone.

"Oh, yes, Mr. Bair," she said. "I've heard a lot about you and your wife." It didn't sound as though she liked what she had heard.

I said, "My wife and I were wondering if you would let us visit the children. It's Christmas, and we have some presents for them."

"All right," she said, "and while you're here maybe you can tell us what's wrong with them. They've been nothing but trouble since we got them."

That was hard to believe. I'd never met two kids more eager to please. "Can we come right over?" I asked.

"Suit yourself," she said.

We went over, taking Jeanne with us. Marty and Ted were at the window as we pulled up. It had snowed heavily and the day was cold, but even before we were out of the car, they came bursting from the house without any wraps on; and with the hugging and kissing and crying, it took some time to get them back inside. We met the couple they were now living with, but the joyful panic of our reunion was out of control, and an hour passed before we could calm the kids enough to play with their new toys while the grown-ups talked.

The couple were pleasant, elderly people who had never had children of their own, and had taken in foster children for company in their old age. I wondered if they hadn't made a mistake in accepting children who were so young. In any event, it was clear that the kids were running them ragged. Marty, it seemed, wet her bed every night. She'd had this problem when she first came to our home, too. After the doctors told us there was nothing physically wrong with her, we gave the only therapy that could be effective with a small child who felt uncertain and insecure: plenty of love.

Ted, it seemed, was forever getting into fights with neighborhood boys. This was unlike him. When we got Ted, he was too frail to have a temper. He gained some weight after his adenoids came out, but even then he had to be anchored down in a high wind. I wondered if Ted was acting up outside the house to let off the steam that built up from living with an elderly couple who liked things pretty quiet. But I wasn't a psychiatrist, and I wasn't about to express an opinion to a couple of nice people whose only shortcoming was that they hadn't had much to do with kids.

The visit was successful enough until Ted and Marty saw us putting on our coats. Then they started howling, worse than on their first day with us. They stampeded us as we went out the door, and actually had to be held back to keep them from following us. They were at the windows, crying, as we drove away.

"Oh, Bill," Marilyn said. "We never should have done it! We've only upset them. It was selfish and cruel of me. But— oh, honey, I've missed them so!"

We'd been back in Aliquippa a couple of days when Marilyn got a call from Bea Love. Bea said she had received an inquiry from the Altoona Child Welfare Department requesting our Aliquippa address. They wouldn't say why.

Marilyn was worried. "I'll bet that couple turned in a complaint about us."

"Maybe."

A week or so later, as I pulled up in front of the house after work, Marilyn dashed out and came running across the lawn. "Bill! Bill! I got a letter! I got a letter! I've been trying to reach you all day."

Before I could speak, she thrust the letter into my hands. It was from the Altoona Child Welfare Department. There had indeed been a report of our visit made by the couple to the department. But it was not a complaint. It was a surrender. After seeing the children with Marilyn and me, the couple had decided that the kids would never be happy with other foster parents, and they had recommended to the department that something be done to have them placed with us in Aliquippa. The department's board of commissioners had held a meeting and voted that, due to the specialness of the case, Marty and Ted would be allowed to return to us if we still wanted them.

I cannot describe what it was like to have Marty and Ted in our car, driving them once again to *our* home. The kids were so happy they couldn't sit still and kept climbing all over Marilyn and me. And that's how I made a discovery. Somehow, perhaps because I was learning to love people through the Lord, my silly hang-up about affectionate boys had simply disappeared, left behind me as I walked up that aisle. I knew suddenly that Ted needed love—overt love—as much as Marty, and for the first time I was able to give it to him.

But it was Marty who threw me the grabber. At one point, she said, "Daddy, promise us that you'll never sell us to anybody else again."

Sudden tears almost blinded me. I said, "Sweetheart, I don't know what the Lord has in store for your mommy and me, but I promise you that you and Ted will be part of it because you are part of us."

I could not know that I had spoken prophecy. I could not know that the Lord had already shown me what He had in store for us. I could not know that it would all come about because of the boy at my side and the girl with her arms around my neck.

# 7

The summer of 1960, the cottages that the Loves, the Harrisons, and we were building on the Jersey shore were complete enough to live in. None of us could afford furniture yet, but it didn't matter. We slept in sleeping bags on the floor and cooked outdoors. Jeanne was still too young to get much out of it, but I'll never forget the expression on Marty's and Ted's faces the first time they saw the Atlantic Ocean. They stood there a long time, staring. "And that," Ted said finally, "is just the top of it."

That August Marilyn said to me, "Bill, I'm working on your birthday present."

"Already? It's not until April."

"I know," she said, "but it usually takes nine months to make one of these things."

I looked at her. "You mean—" She beamed and nodded. "In April?" She nodded again.

I felt a great wave of gratitude to the Lord for blessing our family in this way, performing miracles in Marilyn which the doctors said would never happen. He was blessing us in so many ways. I'd completely lost the desire to smoke or drink. That night as I had walked down the aisle to make my commitment, I hadn't felt that there was anything wrong in these habits, and I certainly hadn't asked the Lord to take them away. This was something the Lord had done for His own reasons, even if they were just reasons of health, and I was grateful to Him for my increased energy and stamina. I was grateful, too, for the end of the convulsions that had kept me living in dread so long; since that night there had not been a single recurrence. I still had the scar: every time I combed my hair I saw it, and thanked the Lord again for what He'd done. But the Lord's blessings were more than just the things He took out of my life. I had asked Him for occasions to love, and He kept pouring them on. My marriage was good. Marty and Ted were back with us. Jeanne was growing into a beautiful little girl. My work constantly put me with people. And now we were going to have another baby.

Christmas Eve we celebrated at home in Aliquippa, just the five of us. Ted was old enough now to earn money doing neighborhood chores, so this was the first Christmas that he was able to give presents that he had paid for with his own money. As excited as he was over the gifts he received, I'd never seen him as excited as he was over the things he was giving. My present was a plastic letter opener. As I opened the package, he hovered over me, watching my face. "Do you like it, Dad? Is it all right? Can you use it at the office?" I told him I could, and I did. After that, whenever Ted came into my office he'd glance at my desk for the letter opener, and, seeing it, he'd nod to himself. The opener became a symbol between us, saying something Ted could not as yet express himself: "I know that you love me. I want you to know that I love you. This opener says it for me. When I'm older, I'll say it better." The years have taught me that children know they are children and cannot perform on an adult level; when they do try to do something, it becomes all the more important for them to know that what they have done is accepted, approved, and appreciated. This way, they feel stronger within the family circle, more worthy of their place at the table, more likely to want to remain in both places.

Christmas Day we drove to Altoona to divide the day between Marilyn's family and mine. Judy—Marty and Ted's little sister—was then in her third foster home, and we were able to spend awhile with her too. I wondered why it seemed impossible for Judy to remain in one foster home for long. She was such an adorable child that I was sure any family would love to have her.

As the winter passed, Marilyn was the one who seemed least concerned about the approaching birth. But this was typical of her. Marilyn had always been a quiet person, a little shy, somehow always disappearing into the background, and yet always the person who was busiest, getting the most done. She wanted no fuss and no special attention during her pregnancies.

On Sunday, April 7, two days before my birthday, instead of starting lunch when we got home from church, she said she'd lie down awhile. I left her alone for an hour and then looked in on her. She had an arm over her face. "Honey," I said, "it's all right with me if my present gets here early. Are the pains starting?"

"Yes," she said.

I called the doctor and gave him the timing, and he said I should call him back in two or three hours. I went out and began to pace the backyard. Our neighbor, Mrs. Rose Demma, called from her back door, "Are you all right, Bill?"

"Sure, Rose. I'm all right."

"You don't look it," she said. "How's Marilyn?"

"Her pains are starting."

"Is there anything I can do?"

"I don't know. Would you take a look at her?"

"Of course." We went into the house. Rose took one look at Marilyn. "Bill, you've got to get her to the hospital!"

"Is it time?" I asked.

"There's *no* time," Rose said. "I've had three kids of my own—I ought to know. Hurry, Bill!"

I said, "I'll have to get a baby-sitter."

"I'll stay with the kids," Rose said. "You get going."

I practically had to carry Marilyn to the car. We were downtown, crossing the bridge, when Marilyn whispered, "Oh, Bill." I looked at her. Her dress was a mess, and there was water on the floor. The wheels screeched as I cut into the hospital driveway. I ran inside. "Somebody help me! My wife is going to have her baby in the car!" Nobody paid any attention to me. I rushed up to the receptionist. "My wife is going to have her baby in the car!"

"You'll have to sign her in first," she said.

I saw a wheelchair down the hall and ran and got it. Then I saw a young man in a white suit. I didn't know whether he was a doctor or an orderly, but I grabbed him by the arm and told him, "You're coming with me."

Marilyn couldn't move. We lifted her into the wheelchair

and pushed her into the hospital. The young man said, "You sign her in. I'll take her up to delivery. It's on the fourth floor."

I filled out the many forms in a fog. Ten minutes later, I suffered the agony of the slow ride in the elevator. On the fourth floor, I saw double doors at one end of the hall. Before I could reach them, a nurse stepped out and asked, "Are you Bill Bair?"

"Yes."

She smiled. "It's a girl. Six pounds. Everybody's doing fine."

I had to wait a few minutes before I could see Marilyn and Joni, so I called home and gave Rose Demma the good news. She put Marty and Ted on the phone. Marty seemed very excited, but Ted asked, "Dad, does this mean Marty and me will have to move again?"

"Move?" I wished I could reach through the phone and hug him. "Ted, you can't move out on me now! With all these women in the house, I'm going to need another man to take care of things when I'm not there."

He thought a minute. "Okay, Dad. I'll take care of everything."

I had no idea that, in fact, we would all be moving very shortly. One day, Wes Cullen called me into his office. "Bill we've bought out another gas company. Would you like to go over and take a look at the place?"

We used his car for the hour's drive. As we waited in the reception room, I noticed a big office off to one side. It must have been forty by sixty feet in size. Wes and I spent couple of hours inspecting the plant, then he led me into that big office and we sat down on leather chairs.

Wes asked, "What do you think of the place?"

"It's terrific."

"How'd you like to move in?"

I looked at him. "What are you talking about?"

"Just what I said. How'd you like to move into this office?"

"What as?"

"Sales representative."

I stared at him. "When do I have to make up my mind?"

"Why not make it up right now?"

"Because I'd like to talk to my wife about it."

"I'm sure Marilyn wouldn't tell you to turn down a promotion."

"No, I guess not."

"Then it's yes?"

"I guess so, Wes. At least I can give it a try."

Marilyn was thrilled. "You're an executive," she said. "I married a ditch digger who turns out to be an executive."

So again we set out house hunting. When nothing was available in Grove City, we tried other towns nearby. We especially liked New Wilmington: it was small and attractive; the people were friendly. But there wasn't a realtor in the area who had a house for sale.

Then one day as we were leaving New Wilmington along Neshannock Avenue, we saw a man nailing a FOR SALE sign on a big white house that stood on almost an acre of land. Some people might say it was luck, but Marilyn and I knew this was God's place for us—though why we should need such a big one we had no idea. The house had twelve rooms, including a completely finished third floor. There was a huge patio on the roof of a two-car garage, and a backyard almost the size of a football field.

We hadn't been in our new home long when Marilyn called me at my plush, big office one day. "Bill, our family is growing by leaps and bounds."

"You mean—you're starting another present?"

"No," she said. "This child is coming ready-made. The caseworker in Altoona called today. She wanted to know if we would take Judy as a foster child."

"You said yes, I hope?"

"Of course."

So Judy joined our family, and with her arrival it seemed that life could hold no more. Five beautiful kids, summers at the seashore, work I liked, above all the Lord Himself. Little did I think what changes He had in store, or that the changes would begin within a stone's throw of where we were living.

Just down the street from our new house was the Neshannock Presbyterian Church where the pastor was Dr. Victor G. Dawe. For two or three years we knew Dr. Dawe only as the rather austere figure in the pulpit, the occasional Sundays when we'd go to church there.

So it came as a surprise when he called me one day and asked if I could meet him in his office at the church that evening. I had always taken Dawe for a fastidious man, but I changed my mind when I saw that office. Books, magazines, extracts, and correspondence were piled all over his desk and on every flat surface in the room. Another surprise was when he called me by my first name.

"Bill, have you ever heard about spiritual healing services?"

"The Pentecostal type?"

"*You* can call it that. I wouldn't."

"I remember when I was a boy, there was a Pentecostal church near our home; whenever I'd pass the church and hear the singing and the handclapping and the moaning and groaning, I'd cross the street, just to be on the safe side."

"All healing services are not like that. I wrote my doctoral dissertation on the healing ministry in the Early Church. I believe the ministry was valid then, and I believe it is valid now. I've been doing a lot of thinking about it since I've been here, and now I'm certain that this is what the Lord wants me to do. My session has given me permission to start having healing services at the church. Bill, would you help me with them?"

"What could I do?"

"I don't know what's going to happen, so I can't answer that. But I'd like to give it a try and I'd appreciate your support, Bill."

"When will the first service be?"

"A week from Sunday evening. I'll make the announcement next Sunday morning."

"I'll be there."

When I told Marilyn she was disturbed. "I wish you wouldn't," she said. "You know how I feel about that."

"I'm not going to take part in it," I said. "I'm just going to help the man out."

"What are you going to do? Chop up discarded crutches for kindling?"

"That's not nice," I told her. "I don't believe in this Pentecostal business any more than you do. But I couldn't refuse the man a favor."

For the first few months, the healing services were well attended. Many were curiosity seekers, people hoping to witness miracles—miracles without faith. The premise on which Dr. Dawe operated, he used to say, was that Jesus wanted to heal the whole man—body and mind and soul—not to effect physical healing alone. Also, most of the individuals who went forward had ailments like arthritis, high blood pressure, or migraine headaches, so cures could not be readily observed.

Because of the lack of drama, the attendance dropped off. Actually, if there was a show to watch, it was Vic Dawe himself. As he moved among the people who had come forward for prayer, he was a completely different man from the one people saw on Sunday mornings. He would say, "Praise the Lord!" and cry out, "Thank you, Jesus!" It was a Vic Dawe most of his parishioners knew nothing about.

Present every month were about twenty men and women who were what Vic called Charismatics—the spiritually endowed. They always stayed after the healing service and went to a room across from Vic's office to hold their prayer meeting. Often as I was leaving I'd glance in. Nothing very unusual seemed to be happening. Sometimes they'd all be standing in a circle, holding hands, their heads bowed, and from the strange sounds, I assumed they were praying in tongues. Other times they'd be sitting in a circle of folding chairs, maybe singing a hymn, maybe just sharing. At times I was tempted to join them, but then I would think about the Pentecostal meetings that sent me to the far side of the street when I was a boy back in Altoona.

One Sunday evening—it was March 7, 1965—Vic had asked Cosmo DeBartolo, a Spirit-led construction contractor, to lead the singing and speak briefly at the healing service. While Cosmo was speaking, I found myself punctuating his remarks with an occasional "Amen" or "Praise the Lord"—just like I had heard Vic Dawe do. I didn't realize I was disturbing anyone until a young Westminster College student—Bob Ledwith—turned in the pew in front of me and shot a withering glare in my direction.

When the service was over Vic invited any who were interested in a deeper walk in the Spirit to stay for what he termed a "prayer and praise" session. About twenty of us gathered in the smaller room. Cosmo talked quietly for about thirty minutes longer. His earnestness and love reached out and touched all of us. The noise, the moaning and groaning that I half expected, was conspicuously absent. Only an occasional whispered "Thank You, Jesus" or "Praise God" escaped the lips of the others as Cosmo continued to talk about the spiritual gifts that awaited us.

Those in the room who had already experienced the Holy Spirit Baptism now began speaking in tongues and laying hands on the others. From various parts of the room came the joyous sounds of praise in a new language as one after another surrendered his voice and his inhibitions to the Spirit. I yearned to join the chorus and yet I couldn't quite let go.

A strong arm across my shoulder and the sound of someone praying in the Spirit close to my ear startled me. It was Bob Ledwith. Christ had Spirit-baptized him that night and his first desire was to pray for me—the guy who less than an hour ago had irritated him no end.

I could hold back no longer. My spiritual language seemed to blend in perfect harmony with Bob's as we embraced each other. For the first time I knew the real meaning of "Praise the Lord."

It was after eleven when I got home. I heard Marilyn's voice on the phone upstairs. "Bill," she called, "pick up the phone in the kitchen. It's John. He wants to talk to you about the cottages."

I picked up the telephone. John Love's voice sounded excited. "Listen, Bill, I was wondering what you'd think—"

I cut in. "Hey, John, guess what happened to me tonight? I got the Baptism of the Holy Spirit."

There was a click on the upstairs phone. The next minute Marilyn was standing in front of me, furious. "I don't think that was one bit funny."

"I'm serious, honey. Wait till I tell you!"

"You know how John feels about all that. I think you ought to apologize."

But John, apparently, was so wrapped up in his own news he hadn't heard mine. "I think the deal sounds good, Bill," he was saying. "I think we ought to talk to them." We had been renting the seaside cottages for three years and were doing very well, so well, in fact, that we'd been thinking of building a few more cottages in Jersey and even of buying land in Florida where we could build. That night, John had heard about some available land south of Daytona. It was a long conversation and nothing more was said about the baptism. By the time I went upstairs the lights were out and Marilyn was in bed. I was sure she wasn't asleep, but I could see that this was not the moment for a talk.

The next day dawned warm and bright, so we had breakfast out on the patio. When everyone was finished, I picked up several plates, went into the kitchen, and started running the water.

Ted came in with some dishes and asked, "Dad, what's got into you?"

"What do you mean, son?"

"I've never seen you wash dishes before."

"Enjoy the sight," I said. "You may not see me do it again." When Judy came in with the cups I told her, "Honey, set up the vacuum cleaner in the front room for me, will you?"

"Mommy," I heard her report to Marilyn in awed tones, "Daddy wants to run the *vacuum cleaner.*"

I heard Marilyn laugh. It was the first sign of life out of her all morning. Without sulking, she had been pretty silent. I knew she was waiting for an explanation about the baptism, but I figured the best thing was to wait until she asked for it.

I was so happy in my new relationship with the Lord that each day was like a gift straight from Him. Any opportunity to be of the slightest service to anyone made me feel great. Despite the unmentionable subject between us, Marilyn and I were getting along well. Sunday evenings, when I would leave early for the healing service and come back late after the prayer meeting, she never said a word. I was only sorry that this wonderful experience in my life was something I could not share with her.

The baptism had given me a great hunger for the Bible, and I started reading it every spare minute. I didn't have much difficulty with the New Testament, but I was lost in most of the Old. Vic Dawe began filling me in on the Bible history I lacked. He loaned me books to read and we had long talks.

Three months after my baptism, I came home one Sunday night and found Marilyn still up, reading in the living room. "Okay, Bill," she said, "you win."

"Win what?"

"I want the baptism."

I couldn't believe it. "You're kidding."

"No, I'm not. I want it."

I sat down opposite her. "Marilyn, you don't have to do this just for me. It wouldn't be right."

"I'm not thinking about you. I'm thinking about myself. Bill, for the past months you've been more loving and more lovable than I've ever known you. You're a changed person, Bill, and I know the baptism has something to do with it. If it's changed you this way, I want it, too."

"What about John?"

"Never mind about John. What do I have to do, Bill?"

"Well," I said, "I suppose the best thing is for you to come to the next meeting. Since I've been going, at least a half a dozen people have received the baptism."

"How does it happen?"

"We just gather around the person and pray for him."

"Can't we do that now?"

"Here? Now? Just with me?"

"Why not?"

I thought about it. I didn't know why not. I'd always supposed there should be a group, but of course the baptism came from Jesus, not the people, however many there were. "We can try," I said.

Marilyn knelt down beside the chair. I placed my hands on her head and began to pray, asking the Lord to give her this beautiful gift of the baptism in His Spirit. I have no idea how much time passed; all I know is that all at once Marilyn began to pray in tongues. I stepped away from her. She was oblivious to me, to everything, except her newfound joy in Jesus. Despite the hour I went to the phone and called Vic Dawe to tell him what had happened. Then I went back to my wife and knelt beside her and together we praised the Lord.

Early in our experience as parents Marilyn and I had made it a rule that the two of us would spend half an hour a week privately with each child, just talking. We never had any specific subjects to discuss, yet we discussed everything, settling problems, solving life's mysteries, guiding, correcting, congratulating, as each was called for. It was during these private sessions that the children, one by one, came into the baptism.

Also, without planning it, it developed that our closest friends were people who had received the baptism. Some of them were people we met in the prayer group; others we heard about and got in touch with. I'll never forget the day John Love asked me to help pray him and his wife Bea into the baptism.

Another day I'll never forget was the first time the Lord spoke to me in an audible voice. I was driving along Route 18 from New Wilmington to Newcastle for a business appointment when a storm came up. Dark clouds closed in and wind started to blow. And then I heard: *Bill, remember, all things are possible by Me.* The voice was so real, so distinct, that I actually stopped the car and looked in the backseat. Of course there was no one there. But I was sure I hadn't imagined it. Someone had spoken, and with a racing heart

I realized who could be the only One to make a statement like that.

A couple of months after this experience, Vic Dawe announced in church one Sunday morning that the church would hold a spiritual-life mission the following week and that the preacher would be the Reverend Leonard Evans from Toronto, Ontario.

Next Sunday, a breakfast was held for the men at our church, a sort of kickoff for the mission. About a hundred of us were there. Leonard Evans spoke on the theme "As you did it to one of the least of these my brethren, you did it to me." His point was that if we considered ourselves Christians we should make service to those who were down and out a regular part of our lives. I thought about this and I realized I hadn't associated with anybody who was really down and out since Georgie White in my boyhood.

That night Marilyn, the five kids, and I went to the opening service, and it was wonderful. Next morning at work, I canceled all evening appointments for the rest of the week. Each night, Leonard Evans spoke on a different aspect of love. He talked about the love between husband and wife, between parents and children, the love of friends and neighbors. I could see that there certainly was a lot of love coming my way, but I was also beginning to find out that there wasn't much love going out of me to others. I knew I had to do something about it.

Friday came. The night was cold; there was snow in the air. The Bair family bundled up warmly for the two-block walk to the church. There was a good crowd, but all seven of us were able to find seats in the same pew, about a quarter of the way down the aisle. At half-past seven, Vic Dawe and

Leonard Evans came out. Dawe led the congregation in singing "Since Jesus Came Into My Heart." Since my baptism, I'd enjoyed singing in a new way. At home, a couple of nights a week the whole family would gather around our electric organ and sing hymns as Marilyn played, and it seemed the room would just be flooded with the love of God. After the hymn, Vic read off some announcements about the closing meeting the following night; then he said a prayer and the offering was taken. After this, Leonard Evans stepped into the pulpit.

He was about three minutes into his sermon when something strange began to happen to me. I seemed to be losing my hearing. Evans's voice became softer and softer until I couldn't hear him at all. I was aware of the people around me, of Marilyn at my side, and yet I had the oddest feeling that I was actually somewhere else. I was plenty scared. And then I heard:

*Bill, I want you to work for Me.*

It was the voice I had heard in the car.

"Lord Jesus?" I whispered under my breath.

*I want you to work for Me.* The words were so clear I wondered that the people around me didn't hear them. I glanced at Marilyn. She was giving Leonard Evans her full attention.

"Gosh, Lord, I—I do work for You, don't I—helping Vic out on Saturdays? And, ah, the teen-age class I'm teaching now on Sunday!"

*I want you full time.*

I swallowed. "Lord, You know I've got a full-time job for the gas company in Grove City. I have about all the job a guy like me can handle."

*I want you to quit the gas company.*

Quit the—now I knew I was imagining things. "For a minute, Lord, I almost thought I heard You say to quit my job! Why, with Ted almost ready for college, and the mortgage on the house, and everything, I need that job like never before!"

*And I want you to sell the beach cottage.*

Sell the cottage? The place where we had such great family times? The place we talked about and looked forward to all winter? "Lord, I wouldn't mind so much for myself, but I've got to think of the kids."

Think of the kids. . . . Suddenly, without knowing how it happened, my mind seemed crowded with faces—young faces—not only the faces of our own youngsters, but ones I'd never seen before. Sad faces, rebellious faces, frightened faces.

*Look at them, Bill. My children are not wanted. My children have nowhere to go.*

"And You want Marilyn and me, someday, when I retire, maybe, to start some kind of program for kids like this?"

*Not someday, Bill. Now. I want you to quit your job now.*

"But how will I support my family? How will I support this program I'm supposed to start?"

*I will provide.*

"Look, Lord, I've worked eighteen years for the gas company. In two more years, I'll be eligible for a pension. Just two years! We could set up a lot better program with some regular income coming in."

*Do you think I can't provide for My workers as well as the gas company does? I want you to quit your job now.*

"Lord, I just can't walk out on the gas company. They've been too good to me. I'd have to give them notice."

*Give them notice, then. And one thing more.*

"Just don't ask me to leave my wife."

*I want you to stand up in front of this congregation and tell them what you're going to do so there's no backing out.*

"But what about Marilyn and the kids? I'd have to consult them first!"

*Now.*

I looked around desperately, wishing the door were a few feet closer. "Lord, if all this is really You, You know I'd do anything. But what if I'm just imagining things? What if these are just crazy ideas from my own head? I don't know if this is all right to ask, Lord, but, if this is You, could You give me a sign?" I thought quickly. "Lord, Leonard Evans is up there preaching. He doesn't know. me. We only met once, Sunday morning, and he shook hands with about a hundred people. If this is You, Lord, have Leonard Evans say my name. Have him say it right now, from the pulpit. Then I'll do everything You said."

I settled back in the pew feeling safely out of a bad situation.

Something was poking me in the ribs. I looked at Marilyn. She nudged me with her elbow again. "Bill, what's the matter with you? Leonard Evans has spoken to you twice. Answer him."

I stared up at the pulpit. Leonard Evans was looking straight at me. "Is that right, Bill Bair?" he said. "Do you agree with me?"

"That's right, Mr. Evans," I managed to croak out, though I didn't have the faintest idea what he'd been talking about.

Oh, Lord, Lord, I was thinking, it *was* You! And now—what had I got myself into? What had I promised? First of all, to stand up in front of this whole church. . . .

"Not yet, Lord," I begged. "When he gives the altar call." Every night dozens of people had gone forward at the close of Evans's sermon. "I'll go up when the others go and I'll tell the people nearest me. That will count, won't it, Lord? Will that be okay?"

It seemed to me that Leonard Evans had never given a more stirring call than he did that night. I waited for the trek forward to begin; I didn't want to be the first.

In that entire church, not a soul budged.

Evans repeated the call. In growing puzzlement he pleaded, he insisted, he practically demanded. No one stirred.

And so at last I made the long walk forward alone, as God had told me to. At the front I turned around and, speaking as rapidly as I could, said I was quitting my job and selling my Jersey cottage and starting a home for kids and would they please pray. Then I turned and faced the altar because I couldn't meet the eyes of my family.

I heard footsteps coming down the aisle and then I felt a hand in mine. It was Marilyn. "Bill," she said, "I have no idea what's going on, but I'm with you all the way."

Now there were other footsteps, and sounds of weeping. We turned around. All five of our kids were standing there and they were all crying—whether because they'd lost the cottage or for some other reason, I didn't know. Behind them some thirty or forty people had also come forward, many of them weeping.

Vic Dawe came down the altar steps and took my hand. "Bill, you just tell us how we can help you and we'll do anything."

"I'm mighty grateful, Vic," I said. "The problem is the Lord hasn't told me yet what *I'm* supposed to do."

# 8

The weekend passed in excitement and confusion. The telephone and the doorbell rang constantly with people wanting to help, and I grew increasingly embarrassed at having to confess that I did not have a very clear idea what they'd be helping with.

For the moment what worried me most was this business of quitting my job. At first I thought I could just go to the office on Monday and dictate a letter of resignation. That would be the easy way. But I knew at once it would also be the wrong way. The men who were my supervisors had been my friends for many years; I owed it to them to go to them personally and tell them the truth, however ridiculous and farfetched it might sound.

Monday morning at six o'clock I was pacing the living-room floor. I knew that the devil could do everything that the Lord could do except forgive sin, and suddenly I was wondering whether, out of some kind of spiritual egotism, I had only talked myself into believing I had heard the

Lord's voice on Friday evening. I was scared stiff, chiefly about how I would ever support my family. I longed to forget the whole thing, and just go on as before. So I'd made a spectacle out of myself at church on Friday—eventually the excitement would die down and the whole thing would be forgotten. I had never been in such a quandary.

I wandered out to the kitchen. Without thought or decision, I took the wall phone off the hook and dialed Jack Hoey, my boss, at his home in Pittsburgh. I heard his phone ring several times before his sleepy voice answered. "Hullo?"

"Jack, it's Bill Bair. I apologize for calling you at this time of the morning."

"Bill Bair? Is anything wrong, Bill?" I heard his wife say something in the background but I didn't catch it.

I said, "Not really. Jack, will it be possible for me to see you today?"

"I don't know, Bill," he said. "My schedule is pretty full. Is anything wrong?"

"No, Jack, nothing's wrong. But something has come up, and it's important to me."

"Then okay, Bill. I'll make time. Come in around two this afternoon."

When I got to Jack Hoey's office in Pittsburgh, with him were Bob Pettigrew, who had succeeded Wes Cullen at Glenshaw, and Glenn Conley, who had Bob Pettigrew's old job. We all shook hands and then we sat down and Jack asked, "Okay, Bill. What is it?"

I said, "Jack, I'm quitting my job."

He said, "I'll be darned! This morning, when my wife heard it was you calling, she said, 'Bill Bair is quitting the gas company.'"

"She must be clairvoyant," I said.

He shrugged. "I always knew she could read my mind but I didn't know she could read anybody else's. Anyway, that's why I asked Bob and Glenn to be here, just in case. What's wrong, Bill? Are you unhappy out there for any reason? Is it the money?"

"Nothing's wrong," I said, "and I never earned better money in my life. It's just that I'm going into another line of work."

"What line?"

"I'm going to work for the Lord."

There was a pause. Then: "Can't you work for the Lord and the gas company at the same time?"

"I thought I could," I said, "but the Lord said no. The Lord told me to quit my job." I caught the three of them glancing at each other.

Jack Hoey cleared his throat. "Well, Bill, I mean, you've been with the company a long time. We're all your friends here. Would you—ah—would you mind giving us the details behind all this?"

So I told them everything.

Afterward, Glenn Conley was the first to speak. "Bill, I'd sure hate losing you. You know I'm new in the territory, and you're the most experienced man I've got."

"Glenn, any time you need me all you have to do is call. I'll always be glad to help out in any way."

He said, "Thanks, but let me make my point. I hope you don't think that the Commonwealth of Pennsylvania is going to let you just open up some kind of a house and start packing it with kids off the streets. There are all kinds of regulations about these things. You'll probably need to set up some kind of foundation."

I said, "The Lord already told me that."

"He did?"

"Yesterday morning at church. He said, 'Bill, I want you to set up a foundation.' And I said, 'Lord, I don't know anything about setting up a foundation.' And the Lord said, 'You just take the first step and I'll do the rest.'"

Bob cleared his throat. "Well, Bill, the first step is to get a charter. Do you know how long it takes to get a charter in this state? I never heard of any outfit getting a charter in less than eight or nine months, usually a lot longer."

"I didn't know that," I admitted.

Jack asked, "What about staff?"

"The Lord said He would provide."

"Have you got a place to put all these kids you'll supposedly find?"

"No."

They all looked at each other again. Jack said, "I think we've all got the same thing on our minds. Bill, you're jumping the gun. Okay, so you had this experience Friday night. Now first thing you want to quit your job. I think you ought to give the Lord a little time to start coming through on some of these promises of His before you go off the deep end. If you want my advice, you'll stay on the job until you've got this other thing going. You know the company will let you have time off for it whenever it's necessary."

I said, "But the Lord didn't put it to me that way, Jack. He said I should quit my job."

Bob said, "Bill, I don't mean to say that I doubt what

you've told us, but, well, how can you be sure you're doing the right thing?"

I said, "Because when I think of disobeying the Lord I feel miserable and when I think of obeying Him I feel marvelous."

When I got back to New Wilmington, I met with Thomas Mansell, a local attorney, and discussed the need for a charter with him. He said, "Bill, I want to be part of this."

I said, "I'd appreciate that. We'll need a lawyer. Only we don't have any money for a retainer."

"Forget that," he said. "I won't charge you for my services."

The next day, Marilyn, the kids, and I drove to Altoona to tell our families what had happened. The hardest part was telling the Loves that we had to sell our share in the cottages; our two families and the Harrisons had had such great times there. I could see our kids were pretty near tears again. But to our surprise John Love said, "Y'know, Bill, I've been thinking of selling, too."

"You have?"

"Yes. Lately I've gotten interested in breeding calves for veal. I've read a lot about it and there's a lot of money in it. I've been thinking of going into that when I retire next year, and of buying a farm somewhere around here. But to do that, I'd have to have the money from the cottages."

"John, you sound serious," I said. "When do you think you'll make up your mind about it?"

He smiled. "I just did. If you're selling, so are we."

Together we went to the Harrisons, who decided they could use the cottages as an investment. By the end of the afternoon all the arrangements had been made. Things move fast when they're going God's way.

Friday I had a dental appointment. I had known Dr. Tom King for two years, so when he asked me what was new, I told him. As he listened, I could see that something was on his mind. When I finished, he asked, "Bill, have you found a place yet to put these kids when you start taking them in?"

"No."

"Just a minute," he said. "I want you to talk to my brother." Dick King was also a dentist. He came in and listened to my story, his expression asking why this was important enough to take him away from a patient. "What about the farm?" Tom prodded him.

"What about it?" Dick asked.

"Bill's going to need a place to house these kids."

Dawn broke on Dick's face. "Oh, yeah!"

I asked, "What farm?"

Dick said, "Bill, a few months ago, five other doctors and I bought a hundred-and-ninety-acre farm a few miles out of town. Now we don't know what to do with it. Would you be interested in buying it?"

"Does it have a house on it?"

"Yes, a big one—four bedrooms, big living room, big dining room."

"I'd be interested all right," I said, "but I don't have any money. Would you rent it?"

"I don't know," he said. "Let me check that out." During the fifteen minutes Dick King was gone, I prayed hard, asking the Lord to have His way in this and also to keep my mind off Tom King's instruments as he began to fill my mouth with them. Dick came back. "It's okay, Bill. You can rent the farm."

"How much?" I said around the cotton swabs.

"Eighty-five dollars a month," he said. "And because you'll be using it for a children's home, we've agreed to cover the heating expenses."

After that, nothing that Tom King could do could take my mind off my gratitude to God.

That evening I had promised Victor Dawe to go with him to the Youngstown Full Gospel Businessmen's meeting to tell about my experience in church the week before. In my talk I mentioned being offered the farm. As I headed back to my seat, I passed the next speaker on his way to the podium, a Methodist minister who looked very much down at the mouth. "Is something the matter?" I whispered as we passed.

He sighed. "The Lord just spoke to me, and now I have to pay your rent on that farm."

I was amazed. "Thank you very much!" I stammered.

"That's all right," he said, still slightly disgruntled. "I just can't figure out why it is that every time the Lord speaks to me it costs me money."

The next Sunday night I spoke at a little country church in Volant. After the service, a man came up and introduced himself as Arthur Snyder, and said that the Lord had just told him to pay the electricity bills at the farm. I was still thanking him when another man stepped up and said he was Charles Wyatt and that the Lord had told him to cover the farm's telephone bills. I was still unused to the speed and perfection of the Lord's provision. It was less than a

118 Love Is an Open Door

week since I had admitted to my boss that I had no place
in which to do the work I thought God was giving me.

And now we had a farm, all expenses paid.

It was November when a caseworker phoned from the
Lawrence County Welfare Office. She wanted to know how
soon would we be getting our charter. They had an emergency. Jimmy, at nine, had become so incorrigible that he
was no longer allowed in school. His parents were separated
and he was living with his grandmother, who could no longer
control him. This didn't sound like much of a prize to me
but I checked with Marilyn. To my surprise, she was all for
him. "This is the kind of child God showed you, remember?
The ones others have given up on—the ones nobody wants.
Bill, we don't have to wait for the charter, or for the farm
to be ready! We can bring him here—we're approved as a
foster home already."

Jim and the caseworker arrived at half-past two the next
afternoon. The boy was about four feet tall, skin and bones,
dirty, his clothes in shreds. The caseworker had to push him
from behind to get him through the door. Marilyn said,
"Welcome to our home, Jim. We hope you'll be happy with
us."

He didn't say a word. I said, "You look like you could use
some cookies and milk. Let's go out to the kitchen and let
the women talk." He didn't say anything, but as I headed
for the kitchen he followed me. In the kitchen was the picnic
table we kept out on the patio in the summer. Jim sat down
on the bench. He sampled the milk I set before him. He ate
a cookie. Then he began banging his rubber heels on the
linoleum, leaving black scuff marks. I said, "Now, Jim, when
you finish your cookies and milk, there's a bucket and a

scrub brush in that closet and here are the soap flakes. You'll have to clean up those marks."

"I won't do it."

"I have some news for you," I said. "All the people who live in this house work together to keep the place nice and clean. That's the way we like to live. It is also the way we earn the right to our room and board. You've just lost yours." I took the cookies and milk away from him and was putting the cookies back in the jar when I heard footsteps behind me, heading for the closet.

"Hot water or cold?" he asked.

"Hot," I said.

"Have I got my rights back?"

"You sure have, Jim," I said, heaping the cookie plate high again.

He was just finishing the floor when Jeanne and Joni came in from grammar school. The girls took to him right away, and soon they were wandering all over the house getting acquainted. Repeatedly, I heard Jim say, "You wanna bet? You wanna bet?" I think he meant to sound threatening, but his tone struck me as defensive. Apparently feeling disliked by everybody, he must have felt that he had a lot to prove to himself.

Then Ted came in from high school. He was sixteen then and had shot up to six feet in height. I could hear him and Jim sounding each other out. "What's your favorite sport?" asked Ted.

"I don't go for sports."

"That's too bad," said Ted. "I was hoping you'd be somebody I could work out with."

"At what?" asked Jim.

"Track."

"You a runner?"

"Yes. I'm on the team at school."

"I like to run."

"Good. We'll work out in the morning. You can pace me."

Just then Marilyn stuck her head around the kitchen door.

"Ted, we're low on milk. Will you go to the store and pick up a gallon?"

"Sure, Ma," Ted said, and then, "Hey, Jim, should we put on our sneakers and run it?" It was three long blocks.

"Okay." And Jim produced his first smile of the day.

Over dinner, I asked, "Marilyn, have you decided on the sleeping arrangements? Where will you put Jim?"

Ted said, "Gosh, Dad, I was expecting Jim to share my room. We have so much to talk about."

I looked at Jim. His eyes were on his plate, but his cheeks were deep pink in a blush of pleasure. Several times during the rest of the meal, I caught Jim studying Ted askance, and I knew that the boy had found his first hero.

Jimmy had been with us a few days when his teacher called to tell me that three girls had complained that he had hit them. When Jim returned from school, he came in by the back door; by now he felt enough at home to help himself to cookies and milk. I went out to the kitchen. "Hey, Jim, I didn't know you were a sissy."

He glanced at me. "I ain't a sissy."

I said, "Your teacher called today. She said you hit three girls. Is that true?"

"Yes."

"Why did you hit them?"

"I don't like them."

"If you don't like people, you stay away from them. You don't hit them, especially girls. Are there any boys at school you don't like?"

"Yes."

"Have you hit any of them?"

"No."

"Why? Because you're afraid they'll hit you back?"

"I'm not afraid of anybody."

"I'm glad to hear that. Now, Jim, I don't want you fighting boys, except when you have to defend yourself. And I don't want you ever again to hit a girl, for whatever reason. Now go get the Ping-Pong paddle that's in the middle drawer of my desk."

"You want me to get it right now?"

"It will be better for you if you do." He got up from the table and went through the house to the small room I used as an office. In a moment he was back with the paddle. I said, "Do you know what's going to happen to you?"

"You're going to hit me."

"Right. I'm going to hit you once for each girl you hit. And if you keep on doing that, I'll keep on doing this. Does that sound fair to you?"

"I suppose."

"Now, Jim, those are your new pants and we don't want to damage them. So turn around and drop your pants and bend over." He did. I gave him three good ones, right on the bottom and just hard enough to make a lasting impression.

As he adjusted his clothes, his face was red with humiliation. "I ain't a sissy," he repeated.

"I know you're not, Jim. That's what surprised me. I'm sure we'll never have to have a discussion like this again."

And we didn't.

A few nights later, the caseworker called again, this time around half-past nine. "It's another emergency, Mr. Bair," she said. "A boy, ten, Joey. Both his parents are alcoholics. It's continual combat in that apartment, day and night. I can't let the boy spend another hour there. Will you take him, Mr. Bair, if only for a few days?"

I asked, "Where is the boy now?"

"Here with me in the office. I've got to find a place for him tonight."

"Let me call you back."

All the kids were up so I told everybody what the caseworker had told me. Marilyn said, "I'm surprised you didn't say yes right away, Bill."

"I want the kids to be part of this. How about it?" I asked them. "You'll have to treat him like a brother, you know. Do you want him?" All the kids said yes except Jim, who said nothing. I asked, "What's your vote, Jim?"

He asked, "Where will the guy sleep?"

There was a short silence. "Let's invite him into our room, Jim," Ted suggested. "He can't very well move in with one of the girls, and he might be lonesome all alone on the third floor. I'll bring a bed down from there—but I'll have to leave it to you to look after him."

"I'll do my best," said Jim solemnly.

I called the caseworker. It was almost eleven before she got to the house. We let all the kids stay up so that Joey could meet the whole crowd at once. When I answered the caseworker's knock, I found myself looking down at one of the most attractive kids I had ever seen. He was tiny, blonde, and had big blue eyes and a handsome face that was almost pretty, although it was darkened at the moment by an angry frown. I said, "Come in, Joey."

He took a few firm steps into the house; then he turned, looked up at me, and said, "I want you to know I'm only staying ten days."

"Okay, Joey," I said. "I'm sure we'll have a great time the ten days you're here."

"No, we won't," he said. "You're not going to like me."

"Really? Why not?"

"I'm a mental case," he said. "I should be in an institution."

"Yeah? What's the matter with you?"

"The kids at school call me Jughead."

"What for?"

"Cause my folks are winos. They say I'm going to grow up the same way."

"Do you think you will, Joey?"

"Never. I've tasted that stuff. I hate it."

"Good for you," I said. "We don't like it around here, either. How about something to eat?"

"What've you got?"

"We had baked beans for supper—homemade. And we've got some homemade bread, too, fresh today."

"I'll try some."

I took him out to the kitchen. He ate a big bowl of beans, four slices of bread, and put away over a quart of milk. I didn't know where it was all going, he was so small. And he talked his head off. Everybody had fallen in love with him on sight, and while he was eating the family kept wandering in and out of the kitchen to have a few words with him.

"Ever play baseball, Joey?" Ted asked when it was his turn.

"Yup."

"Are you any good?"

"I'm good," said Joey, "but I have a problem."

"What's the problem?"

"Every time I catch the ball, I wet my pants."

We howled our way up the stairs to bed.

One afternoon I was reading the paper in the living room while the kids romped in the snow in the backyard. Joey's ten days were almost up.

Suddenly the back door flew open and in came Joey, looking like a snowman. Without a pause he came through the house to me, pushed the paper aside, and climbed onto my lap.

"Papa Bair," he said. (Wouldn't you know it? Marilyn and I were Mama Bair and Papa Bair.) "Papa Bair, which comes first, fall or spring?"

"Spring comes first, Joey."

"Well, I want you to know I'm staying till fall."

I was getting worried about the charter. Even preparing the application seemed to be taking forever. We had to cover every eventuality that might arise, without being sure yet just what kind of program ours would be. Marilyn and I felt increasingly sure that the Lord wanted us to include delinquent young people in this work, not just the homeless and neglected, but ones who had actually been in trouble with the law. But taking custody of a child from the courts was a far different matter from accepting a welfare case, and this was what was making the application so complicated.

At last the lawyer was satisfied. And then Dr. Tom King, the dentist, stepped forward. I had forgotten—though the Lord obviously had not—that Tom was also a member of the state legislature. He would take the application to Harrisburg himself, he said, and personally walk it through the labyrinth of red tape.

He left New Wilmington for the capital on December 9. On December 14, I stood in front of our mailbox holding the charter in my hands. I couldn't wait to telephone Jack Hoey at the gas company. I told him, "You said we'd have to wait eight or nine months before anything would happen on the charter. We got it in less than a week."

"Then God must be in this," Jack said.

"I'm sure of that," I said. "Jack, the charter calls for a board of directors. Can I count on you?"

"I would have been hurt if you hadn't asked," he said.

I was able to put together a board of fourteen directors—many of them the men and women who had been standing behind me in the church when I turned around from the altar that Friday night. Leonard Evans also agreed to serve in absentia from Canada. Ever since that night at church Leonard and I had kept in close touch. He'd told me he couldn't account for his having called out my name that way, since he didn't know who I was and had certainly never addressed anyone by name from the pulpit before.

A few days after getting the charter, I had a phone call from him. "Bill, you say you're going to need a professional youth counselor?"

"That's right, Leonard. It's one of the requirements for taking court-awarded kids."

"Well, I've got just the man for you. A young, Spirit-filled Christian who goes to my church up here."

"What's his name?"

"Geert Steenwyk."

"Ah—try that again, Leonard."

"Steenwyk. Geert Steenwyk. He's a Dutchman. He studied at Bible colleges in Holland and England, and he did youth work in Holland for a while. Then he worked for the Big Brothers Organization in Canada, and now he's a youth counselor and a marriage counselor with the county up here."

"How can I get in touch with him?"

Leonard arranged to have Geert call me the next afternoon. Even over the phone I liked him. I liked the way he felt about kids and I liked the way he felt about the role the Lord should have in a kid's life. The first meeting of the board of directors was scheduled for the first of January; I asked Geert if he could come down then to look us over.

Then I asked, "Would you mind telling me what you're earning in your present job?"

"Eighty-five hundred dollars a year," he said.

"See you on New Year's Day," I said.

The charter specifications required the foundation to have a bank account, so Gil Wilson and I had opened one. But there wasn't any money in it. I didn't expect to be seeing much of Geert Steenwyk after New Year's Day.

It was too bad, too, because we all liked him when he came down and I could see he was interested. At the meeting we elected an executive committee; I told Geert that the

committee would discuss a salary offer later. When the committee met the following week, it was difficult to decide on
an offer, in view of the fact that we didn't have any money
in the first place. In the end, we agreed on one hundred fifty
dollars a month, plus board and room. I felt like a fool when
I called Geert in Canada and told him that. I couldn't tell
over the phone how he was reacting. He just said he'd pray
about it and let me know, indicating that his first concern
was for him to be in the center of God's will.

The same day I had a call from Dorothy Taylor. Dorothy
and her husband Bob were retired chicken farmers from
Oklahoma who had volunteered to move out to the farm and
get it going for us. "Bill," said Dorothy, "this place is going
to need a lot of things before it's ready for any children to
move in."

"Like what, Dorothy?" I asked.

"A washer and dryer, for one thing. And a freezer. And
beds. Linen. China and silverware. Kitchen things."

More expenses for that nonexistent bank balance.

In the middle of January, Marilyn and I went to Pittsburgh to visit my sister Elda. While there I also went over
to the gas company to visit friends. In the hall, I ran into
Dick Brown, a fellow gas company salesman, and told him
what we were doing.

He listened with great interest, then said, "Bill, a relative
of my wife just died."

"I'm sorry to hear that."

"She was very old and very ill and we'd been expecting
it," he said. "My point is that she left a big house full of
furniture. My wife's cousin is the only heir and she doesn't
know what to do with all this stuff. She was going to call

the Salvation Army. You can have anything there you like."

The next day, Dorothy Taylor and I were in that house. In the basement we found a washer and a dryer and a freezer. The kitchen was stocked with dishes and silver. The old lady's hobby had been hemming linens, and there were enough sheets and pillowcases and dish towels to supply a department store. And as for beds. . . . The Salvation Army didn't get a thing.

Meanwhile, several weeks had passed and I still hadn't heard from Geert. When a call came from Toronto at last, it was not Geert but Leonard Evans. "Our church elders had a meeting tonight, Bill, and voted to put up Geert's salary every month if he takes the job. He'll be our missionary."

"That's wonderful, Leonard!" I said. "It was a sheer act of faith, offering him even that much. Now if he'll only accept."

Geert did accept; the action by the elders seemed to him one of the signs that this was where God wanted him. But when he arrived in New Wilmington it was evident that something was still troubling him.

About a week after his arrival, he came to see me. "Bill," he said, "you know I brought my car down with me—I couldn't very well do this job without it. What you didn't know was that I still owe seventeen hundred dollars on it. One reason I couldn't decide whether to come or not was that I didn't see how I could keep up the payments on this salary."

I said, "I wish it could be more, Geert."

"Let me tell you what happened last night," he went on. "I had a telephone call from a friend of mine in Canada. He said that for several days he'd felt God was telling him something: he was supposed to take out every penny from his savings account and send it all to me. He called last night to tell me he'd done it. The money is on its way."

"That's wonderful, Geert," I said.

He looked at me evenly for a moment. "Bill, the amount in his savings account was seventeen hundred dollars."

# 9

Even before Geert reached us, we'd taken in our first court-awarded child. David was a fifteen-year-old boy from a nearby small town. I'd heard about him through a Pentecostal minister; David's mother sometimes attended the man's church and occasionally brought David along. But now David was in jail, convicted of stealing a car and facing time in the reformatory. Because of the home situation, David despised his father and, for a year or so, hadn't even spoken to him.

I worried plenty as I drove out to meet David; I wished Geert were here. But the preacher had told me that David wasn't really a bad kid; it was just that he might become one if he weren't taken away from his family and also kept out of the reformatory at this critical point.

The first thing I saw as I stepped into the jail cell was the long hair. This fashion hadn't hit New Wilmington as yet and I knew I could never bring him home like that. The neighbors were alarmed enough already by our plans to take "young criminals" into the program; one look at this mop and they'd be convinced he had arms full of needle holes, and a copy of the *Communist Manifesto* in his pocket. The preacher was there with David, waiting for me. He explained to the boy that there was a chance that I might be able to keep him from going to an institution. David didn't seem much interested. The whole time I was there he was hostile, defensive, curt.

Finally the preacher asked him, "David, do you want to go with Mr. Bair?"

He shrugged. "I don't care."

I said, "Well, before you come to my house, you'll have to get a haircut."

"No one's cutting my hair!"

"They'll cut it for you at an institution," I pointed out.

"They'll have to hold me down."

I changed the subject. "David, why did you steal that car?"

"I wanted to sell it."

"What were you going to do with the money?"

"Give it to my mother. I want her to move out on my father. He beats up on her."

"Have you been going to school?"

"Not much."

"Why not?"

"No clothes. Anyway, school is stupid."

It went like that. He seemed to be resigned to the institution. The preacher said, "Bill, why don't we all think about this for a while? You two have met, so let's take a couple of days to decide how you feel about each other."

"Okay by me," I said. David said nothing. I was pretty sure I wouldn't be seeing this kid again.

But two days later the preacher called me. "Bill, David got his hair cut. That's his answer. What's yours?"

I wasn't sure. "I kind of got the feeling he hated my guts."

"In view of the experience he's had with his father, Bill, you can't expect him to look very kindly on any adult male. For him, men are the enemy—his father, his teacher, the police, even me. And now you. But give him a chance, Bill."

A chance. For me the words always conjured up that morning in the schoolroom and the supervisor who gave me the chance that saved me from spending the rest of my life in fourth grade. "All right," I said. "What's the next move?"

"We'll have to go to juvenile court. There's a session at eleven o'clock tomorrow morning."

With his short hair, David looked like a different boy. He was still hostile and uncommunicative, but I knew that the haircut had been a painful surrender. David's mother was also there. Small and frail, she looked years older than she could possibly have been.

The only plans I had for David, I told the judge, were to keep him at our house for a couple of weeks, then move him out to the farm when Geert got there. He could start high school in the spring term that began in February. If David had any problems that required counseling, I figured Geert would provide that. All I felt qualified for was to try to be a good father to David in every way possible. I also described the foundation and the work we hoped to be doing.

The judge looked at David. "Do you want to try this, David?"

David said, "Yes."

The judge looked at David's mother. "How do you feel about it?"

"Can I visit him once in awhile?" she asked.

I said, "Of course. As soon as David is settled on the farm and gets his bearings, you can visit him whenever you like."

"All right, then," she said.

The judge signed the papers. To David he added, "Remember, son, you're getting a break. Don't goof it. You know the alternative."

I wasn't prepared for the reception David got when he reached home late that afternoon. The four girls were home, plus Joey and Jim, and they took David over before the door was closed behind him. They showed him around the house. They took him for a walk around the neighborhood. When they got back, the girls made cocoa, and they all sat down at the dining-room table over a platter of doughnuts. From my little office off the living room, I could hear them filling David in on the town, school, church, our household routines, the morning and evening prayer sessions, the kids' private half hour a week with Marilyn and me. Without a hint from me, the kids were ministering to David, and I was very proud of them. Bottomless pit Joey said, "Another good thing around here, David, the food is great."

Ted came in, and I heard Marilyn introduce him to David. Right away, Ted said, "Ma, if you'll give me the sheets, I'll go up to the third floor and fix beds for Joey and Jim."

"Hold it a minute," said Joey. "What's the big idea?"

Ted said, "David and I are about the same age. I think we should share a room by ourselves."

"What does age have to do with it?" Joey demanded.

"That's okay, Joey," I heard Jim say, to my surprise. "I'll go up on the third floor with David."

Ted said, "Ma, you'll have to decide."

Marilyn asked, "How about letting David decide?"

"I don't care where I sleep," David said. "I'm only going to be here two weeks, ain't I?"

"You can't tell about that in this house," said Joey. "When I came here, I was only staying ten days."

Marty said, "Why don't you draw straws? Ted can stay in his own room and whoever draws the long straw stays with him."

There was a muddle of excitement as the suggestion was agreed to and the straws broken off the broom—silence during the drawing—then the laughter and the cheers as David drew the long straw.

So David was a member of the family in a hurry. Because of his mother's influence, he was familiar with our way of worship and joined us that evening for our prayer session. The next day, I took him over to the high school and registered him for the next semester, which was to begin in about two weeks. I drove him out to show him the farm and he met the Taylors, and I could see that he liked them. I assured him that after Geert arrived there'd be a whole bunch of kids out there, and I'd be out every day too, in case he wanted to talk to me about anything. Not being in school, David hung around the house most of the time for the following week. He was very helpful to Marilyn, dusting, going to the store for things. Then one day the three of us were having lunch when John Love called from Altoona.

For several years now, the Love and the Bair families had shared a gigantic heartache. Charles, the foster child John and Bea had taken into their home, whom we'd all come to love as one of our own, had been killed in an automobile accident at age eighteen, while hitchhiking between Altoona and Alabama. When I started the foundation, I had asked John Love to serve on the board of directors more out of esteem than practicability; there was still so much sorrow in that house that I didn't expect him to participate much in our activities.

I took John's call in my office. "Bill," he said, "Bea and I have been talking it over. We'd like to have a boy around the house again, a teen-ager."

"I can understand that," I said.

"We were wondering," he went on, "if you happen to have a boy for the Love home."

The Love home . . . a love home. Something about the words struck me.

"Bill?"

I pulled myself out of my reverie. "I'm afraid I don't, John," I began—and then I thought of David. We were expecting three new kids next week from various county agencies; still it was going to be mighty quiet out at the farm until Geert came and we could take the full quota Dorothy and Bob Taylor were preparing for. I told John a little about David—the home picture, the car theft, the impeccable behavior since he'd been with us.

"When can we meet him?" asked John.

It was Thursday. I said, "Why don't you bring the family over tomorrow evening and stay for the weekend? Let's see how it goes. If you like David and he likes you, maybe you can take him home with you on Sunday."

"We'll be there," John said.

I hung up the phone but for a moment I did not leave my desk.

A love home.

What was it in the phrase that seemed to be speaking to me, calling my attention to something I had not grasped?

At last I shrugged my shoulders and went out to the kitchen. Marilyn and David had almost finished lunch. "That was John Love," I said. "He wanted to know if we had a boy to fill the gap in that house. I've invited them for the weekend to meet David. He's Mama Bair's brother, David. They have a terrific place in Altoona."

David said, "And I'd have to go there?"

"It's up to you, of course. But I'm sure you'll like them, David. They're wonderful people."

We finished lunch and I went back to my little office cubbyhole. A couple of hours later Marilyn appeared in the doorway. "Bill, where's David?"

I glanced into the living room. "Isn't he in his room?"

"No."

"Did you try the third floor?"

"Yes. He's not there. Bill, his canvas bag is missing, too. Do you think he's run away?"

I made a quick tour of the house and called his name from the front and back doors. Nothing. I put on a heavy coat: it looked like more snow was coming. I said, "Call John and Bea and have them start praying. Call the Dawes. Call anybody you can think of. And we'd better do some heavy praying ourselves."

"What do you think got into him?"

"I have no idea."

Once I had the car out of the garage I didn't know which

direction to go. Downtown New Wilmington could be searched in detail in ten minutes, so I headed there first. No David. I tried a couple of other roads, then on an impulse drove in the direction of his hometown. Five miles from New Wilmington I saw him, not hitching, just walking, and without a cap. He must have been freezing. I passed him slowly and stopped twenty feet ahead. When he reached the car, he just opened the door and got in. He would not look at me.

I asked, "What's wrong, David?"

"Nothing."

"What happened?"

"Nothing."

"You were all right this morning. Did I say something wrong at lunch? Did I do anything?"

"No."

"Did my wife?"

"No."

"Then why are you running away?"

"No reason."

"That doesn't make sense," I said. "Where were you heading?"

"Home."

"David, if you leave us, you know I'll have to tell the judge. That means the reformatory."

"Maybe that wouldn't be so bad."

"You know better than that." I turned to him. "David, if you want me to drive you to your home, I will. But I think I deserve an explanation. I think I ought to have the chance to understand why you've done this."

"Okay," he said. He looked at me, anger on his face, tears

in his eyes and in his voice. "Tell me—when the judge signed that paper, he turned me over to you, right?"

"Yes."

"So a week passes, and you want to turn me over to somebody else."

"No, I don't."

"You want me to go live with the Loves."

"Only if you want to."

"Why did you change things? You said I could live at the farm. You said you'd come to see me every day. You said if I ever needed you all I had to do was call."

"None of that's changed," I assured him. "Altoona isn't the edge of the world, you know. All right, maybe I wouldn't see you every day, but I get there a couple of times a month, so I'd be seeing you regularly. David, you couldn't find a better family than the Loves."

"What's wrong with your family?" he asked. "Why can't I stay with you?"

"You can if you want to," I said. "But you ought to give the Loves a chance. They're willing to give you one." He didn't say anything. We sat there a minute or two. Then I asked, "David, do you want me to drive you home or do you want me to turn around?"

He thought about it. "Turn around."

When we got home, I could see that Marilyn had been crying, but she covered it up. "You two must be freezing," she said. "Fresh coffee will be ready in a minute. David, why don't you take your bag up to your room?"

When he was out of earshot, Marilyn asked, "What was it?"

"He likes it here. He thought we were trying to dump him."

Marilyn sighed. "Poor kid. You did spring it on us, though, Bill, both of us. So where do we stand?"

"He doesn't have to go to the Loves if he doesn't want to."

"All right," she said. "And Bill, let's not tell the other kids about the running away."

The Loves arrived around six on Friday evening, and I sensed immediately that the whole family was prepared for a big seduction act. David wasn't going to have a chance. There were too many people for a sit-down supper, so Marilyn and the girls had prepared a big buffet. People were eating all over the house, mostly sitting on the floor. Every minute, there was a Love within three feet of David, gripping him in conversation. I caught bits of it. The girls talked to him about school, music, social activities in Altoona. John talked to him about the farm where he was going to raise calves. Bea kept asking him if he was getting enough to eat. Around eight Marilyn went to the electric organ, and for a couple of hours we sang hymns and old songs. A little after ten, we had family worship. At the finish, we stood in a circle, holding hands for the closing prayer, and I noticed the way John and Bea maneuvered themselves next to David. They were pouring so much love into him that I could feel it across the room.

Saturday morning, we had to have breakfast in shifts, and so for a couple of hours the house was filled with the smell of bacon and eggs and sausages and pancakes and coffee and fresh biscuits. The Loves had not seen the foundation's farm. Marilyn telephoned Dorothy Taylor to tell her that we were all coming out for the day and that she shouldn't bother about food because we'd be bringing our own. Then for a long time the house smelled of frying chicken and potato salad in vinegar and pepper-and-pickle relish and new bread.

The day went wonderfully; the weather was cold and clear with no wind. We had snowball fights and went sledding down the hills and skating on the frozen pond. I took on Joey and Jim at checkers, but they kept beating me and I got bored. About four, I suggested to Marilyn that we ought to think about heading home, but Dorothy Taylor said she'd had a big roast in the oven for a couple of hours and that if we didn't stay for supper she and Bob would have to live off it for a month. So we stayed.

Night came quickly. We brought in logs and made a big fire in the hearth, then turned off all the lights and ate by the glow of the fire. Later, the kids made popcorn. It was almost eleven when we got home. We were too tired for anything but a good-night prayer circle, holding hands, and this time, I noticed, it was David who maneuvered himself between John and Bea.

Sunday morning we all slept late, which subsequently meant the battle for the bathrooms, and breakfasts of coffee and Danish before the quick walk to Victor Dawe's church. By early afternoon, heavy clouds had lowered upon us, making the house dark and cozy, in the special way winter has. We had the thick newspapers from Pittsburgh, old movies on TV, visitors, endless touch-tackle football in the deep snow in the backyard, the back door a machine gun of kids after snacks.

Around five, David was suddenly beside me. "Can I talk to you?" he whispered. Before I could answer, he was halfway up the stairs. On the landing, he asked, "When do we have the big discussion?"

"About what?"

"About me going to Altoona."

"There's nothing to discuss, David. The decision is yours."

"I want to go."

"That's fine. You'll be happy with the Loves."

"I know, but will they be happy with me?"

"I'm sure they will. Shall we ask them?"

"No. Wait. I don't want to stand there while people take a vote."

"They won't do that."

"Will you do me a favor?"

"If I can."

"Get Uncle John on the side and ask him if he wants me."

"I'm sure he does."

"I'll wait here."

I went downstairs. John was stretched out on the sofa, the sports section over his face. I sat down, stirring him. Others were in the room, so I spoke softly. I asked, "John, how do you feel about David?"

John said, "I love him."

"Do you want to take him to Altoona tonight?"

"I'm not leaving without him."

"He'll be glad to hear that. He wasn't sure."

I went upstairs. "You're a lucky boy," I told David. "You've got yourself a wonderful family. They're crazy about you."

He beamed. "That's great. You don't mind, do you?"

"Mind what?"

"That I'm going with them."

"Of course not. The Loves are the only family I would let

have you. And it isn't as though we won't be seeing you. We'll all be together a lot."

"That's the best part."

I said, "Now, David, go ahead and pack. But when you come downstairs don't say anything to anybody. Your new dad will pop the news just before you leave."

I went into our bedroom where Marilyn and Bea were visiting. In the voice of a TV commentator I proudly announced, "Bea, you have just become the foster mother of a hundred-and-thirty-pound, very happy baby boy."

Bea's eyes widened. "He said yes?"

"He's already packing. John will announce the birth at six-thirty."

At half-past six, John Love called everyone to the living room. "Okay, my Loves, shall we hit the road?" he asked. "The Bairs have church at seven." There was a stir, the Loves moving to get their things. But before anybody could get far he continued, "David, are you ready to go home, son?"

David said, "Yes, Dad."

A silence.

Then pandemonium, the Love kids cheering, the Bair kids groaning, explanations demanded and given. Still there were mutinous mutterings from my kids as we helped the Loves pack their car and watched them drive away. Only the fact that we had to rush for church saved me being tried and sentenced as an accomplice to kidnapping.

Over the next month or so, I managed to get to Altoona at least twice a month to see David. It was obvious that he was fitting into the Loves' home with no problems. John had purchased the calf-breeding ranch he planned on retiring to, and the big old farmhouse needed a lot of work. Every weekend John and David were out there, putting the place into shape, bragging about how rich they were going to get raising veal.

Meanwhile, the foundation family was growing. We settled the first contingent of six kids out at the farm, welfare cases we were pretty sure the Taylors could handle with their common sense, Dorothy's good cooking, and daily visits from me. Each time it was a wrench to part with them, even as far as the farm, but we had no choice. We were discovering that our house and our kids made a perfect welcome station: a place to relax in, to feel wanted, to get over whatever immediate trauma had brought them to us. But as kids kept coming, earlier arrivals had to make way for newer ones.

Then one morning in April, the very day Geert Steenwyk was due to arrive, the telephone rang. It was John Love.

"David has run away," he said.

"What do you mean? What happened?"

"We don't know," he said. "After supper last night, David said he was going to visit a friend. When he wasn't home by ten for devotions, I called the friend. David hadn't been there and hadn't been expected. He didn't come home all night."

"Maybe you called the wrong friend," I suggested, hopefully. "Maybe he spent the night with someone else."

"No," said John, "he said specifically where he was going. Besides, I just called the high school. He's not there."

"Had anything happened around the house, John?"

"Nothing. Bill, if ever there was a kid who should know he's loved, it's David."

"Did he take anything with him? Any clothes or anything?"

"No."

"You better call the Altoona police, in case he's in the hospital or something."

"All right, Bill. And, Bill, can you come over?"

I said, "Okay, John, but I don't know what time. Geert Steenwyk is due here this morning to take over as counselor. As soon as he shows up, I'll call you and we'll head over."

My main concern about David was that he might get into trouble. Being a court-awarded boy, even truancy could be a serious offense for him. If it was reported to the judge in his home county that he had run away, the judge would take that as proof that the foundation could not control him. Next would come an institution, with all its dangers.

Marilyn telephoned several members of the foundation's board of directors, who in turn phoned others, asking them to pray that the Lord would persuade David to return. Already we had stumbled upon this telephone prayer-chain idea, which was to provide the foundation with its greatest strength over the years. Within minutes of an emergency developing, dozens of Spirit-filled Christians would be at prayer—with results that soon made the word "miracle" a commonplace among us.

Geert pulled into the driveway around noon. When I told him what had happened, he agreed that we should go to Altoona immediately. As we drove along I gave Geert as much information as I had. "If the Loves lose a second son, it'll be very rough on them. David is so much like Charles."

Geert asked, "They resembled each other physically?"

"Not so much that," I said. "In mannerisms. Attitudes. Habits. John and Bea are always mentioning it."

Geert didn't say anything. He just nodded.

We got to the Loves around two. No news of David. At least we had the consolation of knowing that he wasn't in a hospital. Then around three, John Love, standing at the window, said softly, "Here comes David." We all ran to look. He was coming up the block, slowly, dejectedly.

"Listen, everybody, please," said Geert. "Don't make a big scene out of this. Don't scold him, don't demand an explanation. Pretend that he's just coming home from school. Let's sit down and talk about something. Let's talk about your farm, John."

So we all sat down and tried to get a conversation going. David went around the back of the house and came in through the kitchen. He'd been standing in the doorway several seconds before John looked up. "Hello, son."

David said, "Hello."

Bea asked, "Are you hungry, David? Can I fix you something?"

He said, "No, thanks." He was obviously waiting for the assault.

Geert got up. "John, how about introducing me to your son?" As John made the introduction, Geert pumped David's hand. "I'm glad you've come in, David," he said. "We were just talking about your calf-breeding farm. How about taking me out and showing me around?" This was clear out of left field and nobody knew what to make of it. Geert said, "Bill, let's have the keys to your car," and the next minute he and David were out of the house.

They were gone for two hours. When they returned, Geert

sat down, but David didn't. There was something challenging about the way he stood in the middle of the room, facing John and Bea—something manly, in spite of the tears in his eyes. He said, "I came back to tell you that I love both of you. I really feel like you are my parents. I really feel like I'm your son. But I'm your son David. I'm not Charles. Charles is dead. But you keep seeing Charles in me. You act like David died and Charles is still here. I know you don't feel that way, but that's the way you're making me feel. I would like to stay here and live with you, but just as David. Otherwise, I will have to go someplace where I can be myself."

Geert stood up. "Bill, shall we go? We have a lot to do."

As I drove away from the house I turned to Geert. "How in the world did you get him to do that?"

"I didn't," Geert said. "He did it himself. He knew he had to."

"But that's not like David," I insisted. "Running away is more like him. Standing up like that to the Loves is something else."

"If he didn't love them, he wouldn't have done it," Geert said.

"Even so, I'm sure you had something to do with it."

"I just told him about myself," Geert said.

"What about yourself?"

"Well, Bill," he said, "there were two boys in my family back in Holland. My brother was older. He was the scholar, and I lived in his shadow."

"You told this to David?"

"Yes. We were talking about farms in Holland and boyhood in Holland, and I told him how I felt. I thought it would help open him up so he could tell me his problem. I was pretty sure what it was, anyway."

"It sure was lucky that you shared that with him."

"It wasn't luck, Bill," Geert said. "I haven't thought about that until today. Bill, there is no textbook approach to a troubled teen-ager. I've been in this work long enough to know that. When I start on a new case, I forget about what I've read in the files, I forget about what people have told me. I simply ask the Lord to put into my mind what He wants me to do and say. This afternoon, when I saw David coming up the block, I saw 'also-ran' written all over him. Then the Lord gave me the memory of myself at that age. That's when I knew I would have to be alone with him. Telling him about myself would help him find words for what was bothering him. When he did, I told him that the Loves had the right to hear it—from him."

"What do you think is happening at the Loves' right now?"

Geert grinned. "Oh, they're probably all standing around crying and laughing and hugging and making promises. I'm sure this problem's over."

And it was. David stayed with the Loves for almost a year, when a county caseworker felt that David's home situation had improved enough for the boy to return to his family. After about ten days in his former environment, David called John and asked, "Dad, can I come back? I don't think I'm ready for this yet." John cleared it with me, I cleared it with the caseworker, and John drove out to pick David up. David still lives with the Loves.

What we learned with David we were to rediscover time and again in the months that followed, as "delinquent" kids began to be assigned to us regularly from courts and parole boards. We discovered that the teen-ager, despite his efforts at conformity in dress, hair, music, and speech pattern, nevertheless considers himself an individual and wants to be accepted as one. As parents and foster parents, the Loves and the Bairs had known this. But now we were dealing with a different kind of teen-ager, troubled teen-agers, teen-agers in trouble, and we found them to be even more sensitive in this area than ordinary kids, especially if they had ever been in any sort of institution where individualism was considered a kind of rebellion.

We also learned that a troubled teen-ager is most likely to come from a home where there is no father or a weak father. No matter how badly a mother may treat her children, they rarely seem to develop a lasting resentment toward her and, in the long run, usually end up excusing and defending her. Not so the father. Perhaps by some innate awareness of the divine order, children expect the father to be the God-figure in the house—the provider, the leader, the judge, the disciplinarian, the stabilizer, the inspiration. I never met a kid who complained about family poverty because his father couldn't find a job; I met many who complained because their fathers wouldn't try to find a job. Over the years, an axiom appeared: teen-agers—boy or girl—who have a good relationship with their father or the father-figure in their lives have few problems and the resiliency to get over those they do have.

This was especially true in the area of faith. Almost by tradition, the religious training of children in American homes has been left to Mother, with Dad riding along as a spare tire—if that. When the kids get old enough, they leave church behind with their roller skates. We found that where the father fills his role as head of the family's religious activities, when he says his prayers, reads his Bible, leads family devotions, and is active in his church, the children develop a religious life that lasts—however far they may drift away for a time.

By now, we had a bunch of kids out at the farm and another four or five living in our house, which, with the third floor completely occupied and extra beds in every room, was beginning to look like a dormitory. But we had discovered that it was essential to have new kids spend two or three weeks at our home before sending them out to the farm. For practically all of the youngsters, this was their first experience of living in a happy home, a Christian home, and the Bair kids were the key. A doubting, suspicious youngster, especially one who's seen the scruffier side of the adult world, will turn off if a grown-up approaches him; with another teen-ager he will listen, he'll argue—and he'll be more willing to admit it when his own arguments lose out.

The trouble was, there was only so much room in our house, even with sleeping bags end-to-end, and a limit to how many kids we could care for at one time and still be a family.

A family.

And at last the idea that had been staring at me all along broke through the thickness of my skull. A family! That's what every troubled, unhappy youngster needs! A family— to care for him and fuss over him and love him and correct him and let him know he matters. Not a farm or a school or any other program, no matter how high-principled and Christian, but a father and a mother and a couple of brothers and sisters—and some aunts and uncles and grandparents, too.

I thought back to that Friday night in October, ten months and another world ago. When God had shown me those lonely kids, my mind had jumped at once to some kind of building or center. But God had said only, *My children have nowhere to go.* He never said, "Start an institution for them."

What if the farm had only been my own idea? What if God's plan all along had been quite different? What was it John Love had said over the phone last winter? "Do you have a boy for the Love home?" What if private homes, "love homes," had been God's answer from the start? What if the farm had simply been His way of encouraging us until our ears were open enough to hear? In growing excitement I thought of the families I knew right here in New Wilmington who would abundantly qualify as love homes. I thought of the folks who were always asking questions about this work, dropping in to visit, inventing the flimsiest excuses to invite foundation kids out for a soda, a ball game, a ride in the car.

What if, with Geert to counsel and guide the foster families as well as the kids, we were to start sending the youngsters not to the farm when they left our house, but into other Christian homes?

I sounded out Geert and found that the same thought had been haunting him. "Every day I spend at the farm," Geert said, "I realize that eventually it's going to turn into just another organization. No matter how close I get to the kids, I'm not a father and it's not a family. With all those kids under the same roof you just don't get that one-to-one relationship."

Around the kitchen table, Geert, Marilyn, and I talked about the kind of family these kids would need.

First and foremost, they needed a Christian one, where Jesus was an hour-by-hour, moment-by-moment reality—and one where the father took the spiritual lead.

Then, a Spirit-filled family, because with the baptism comes a new ability to love—and such a family would need all the love it could get. Unhappy kids are apt to be unattractive kids, with all kinds of defenses up against a world that hurts, and human love can get pretty frayed within the first twenty-four hours.

It should, in most cases, have teen-agers in it, not only so the parents would have current experience with this age group, but because the teen-agers themselves would be doing so much of the ministering.

And these teen-agers, in fact all the natural children in the family, should be part of every stage of the decision and planning—not only willing but eager to welcome the newcomer among them. This would be no guest arriving for a week or a month, but very often a permanent addition to the household. It would mean, at the least, less space in the house, and for many families, less of the physical extras all around. If the family's own children felt the least bit short of love and attention themselves, if there was noticeable jealousy and competitiveness in the home, it would be no place in which to put an upset and upsetting kid from the foundation.

It sounded like a tall order, and yet in this one small town we soon found five, ten, fifteen families who met all these requirements and a dozen less tangible ones as well—qualities of warmth and humor and understanding crucial to helping people live together.

We began to place kids in these private homes.

If there was a problem in the beginning, it was one of too much kindness, of feeling sorry for the newcomer and excusing behavior they never would have tolerated from their own youngsters. Again and again we had to remind our love home parents that love meant treating the foster child exactly as they did their own, including discipline. Once this hurdle was crossed, the results exceeded even our hopes. One family, for example, took in a boy of fifteen, large for his age. He was a court assignment, faced with a choice of the reformatory or a foster home. He chose the home, but turned it into a kind of jail for himself. He remained quiet and withdrawn, a loner, refusing to take part in family activities. At school, he was lazy and insolent.

One day in math class he wrote some four-letter words on the blackboard and was expelled for a week. His first day at home, he slept late, fixed his own breakfast and didn't clean up after himself, then parked himself in front of the television set. His foster mother came in and saw him. "I hope you don't expect to spend the week like this," she said. "You're not on vacation, you know. You're being punished." He glanced up and muttered an obscenity. She gasped, grabbed him by the shirt, pulled him to his feet, and slapped his face. "The next time you talk to me like that," she said, "I'm going to get a belt!" He stared down at her—he towered over her—dumb with astonishment.

Later, telling me about it, she said, "Frankly, Bill, I was

scared to death. I'd acted on impulse, the way I would if any of my own kids had talked to me like that. But when I got him on his feet and hit him, I realized he could have mopped the floor with me. However, he just stood there, so I brazened it out. I told him, 'Now get your coat and hat. I'm taking you out to my father's farm, and you can shovel manure for a week.' He came along as meek as a lamb."

I asked, "How did he survive the week?"

She laughed. "As it turned out, he loved the farm. Even though my father worked him hard and got him up at dawn with the rest of the family, there wasn't a word of complaint out of him all week. At the end of the time, as I was driving him home, he first apologized for the way he had spoken to me, and then he asked, 'Mom, can I spend my weekends at the farm from now on?' I told him that would depend on how he acted around the house and at school. Well, Bill, he became a new boy. He joined the family, he joined the human race, at school he got interested in Future Farmers, he even stopped griping about church. I think what cured him was the week at the farm—not having so much time to think about himself."

There were benefits to the families, too, that we hadn't expected—like a new pride in their own kids. The foster child inevitably came from a home setup where he hadn't had a chance to study, or wasn't required to, and this showed on his report card. Foster fathers kept saying things to me like, "Y'know, Bill, my boy Pete's a bright kid. I didn't realize how bright until I started comparing his grades with our foster son's. Pete's a budding genius! Now we've got to make this other fellow knuckle down so I can be proud of them both."

The family's own young people, growing up in a stable home with lots of love, pretty much assume this is the way life comes. Then a foster brother or sister moves in, with his experience of irresponsibility or even brutality on the part of parents, and the natural child starts appreciating his folks in a hurry. Appreciation—that's probably the earliest benefit all around, and it's often the foster child himself who puts it into words.

I remember one of the very first love homes, a small place, spotlessly clean if not very fancy. "Even the holes in my linoleum shine," the wife boasted as Geert and I looked the place over. She and her husband had recently received the baptism in the Spirit, and as always happens with the Spirit-baptized, their lives were so flooded with love that they needed something to do with the overflow. We were able to send them a girl of fourteen whose main problem was that her widowed mother was working and could not give her proper supervision after school.

This couple, as I say, was of very modest means; they had a couple of kids of their own, a large mortgage, and a low-priced car. The wife's sister, however, had married a man who became very successful in business. After the foster daughter had been with them for a few weeks, the family accepted an invitation to spend the Labor Day weekend with their rich relatives. The house appeared to them a mansion, with air conditioning throughout, carpets even in the bathrooms, every meal a sit-down affair in the dining room. Late Monday night the family returned to New Wilmington. As they traipsed through the door of their little house the mother said, only half jokingly, "Well, folks, welcome back to the poorhouse."

Everyone laughed except the foster daughter. "Mom," she said, "your sister's place is big, okay, but this—" she waved her hand around the tiny living room—"this is the most beautiful house in the world."

And so it was. All the love homes were beautiful and so were the things happening in them. Every week brought new requests from families who wanted to be part of this work, every week new inquiries from courts and other agencies with children to place. And then the storm broke.

We'd been in operation over a year when one day I got a telephone call from the regional office of the state welfare department. An irate woman demanded to know who we were, what we thought we were doing, and how we dared operate a foster-home program without a charter. I told her who we were, what we hoped we were doing, and that I would be happy to bring our charter to the regional office to show it to her. She said this wouldn't be necessary. She was coming up to New Wilmington to look us over.

This is how we learned that an important step had been overlooked in the course of getting the charter. The pressure which Dr. Tom King had applied on the appropriate state officials to speed our application through the labyrinth of committees, had apparently been so effective that one crucial procedure had been left out altogether. At some point before the final approval, the application should have been sent to the regional headquarters and someone from there should have come to New Wilmington to inspect our facilities and examine the credentials of the staff. Instead, the charter had been mailed directly to us, bypassing the headquarters entirely.

But the financial arrangements did not bypass headquarters. For each child the foundation was paid three dollars a day for room and board, plus ten dollars a month for clothing. Most of this was passed along to the foster families. It was never enough, of course, but the families were not taking in kids for profit, and they willingly dug into their own funds to make up the difference. In addition, I was giving talks to churches and business clubs which often resulted in donations. With these gifts I paid the foundation's bills, met the expenses of our own bulging household, and was usually able to give a few dollars a month pocket money to each of the foster children. But meanwhile, the county welfare agencies were being reimbursed each month by the regional office, where nobody knew we existed. When the dawn broke, it brought its thunder.

The inspector was not friendly. She inspected our house and admitted, a little grudgingly I thought, that it was a suitable residence for foster children. Then she asked to see my office and files. I breathed a prayer of sheer gratitude that this was no longer in the little alcove off the living room. We'd been acquiring so many records that the little room had been swamped in paper, with card files under the desk and the chair straddling the letter basket. The thought had occurred to me to convert our two-car garage into office space, but there was no money for such a project. Then one day an elderly man had come to the house. He was too old, he said, to take a foster child into his home, but he wanted to know if there was any other way he could help the foundation. When he mentioned that he was a retired carpenter, I told him about my idea for the garage. Not only did he design the suite of rooms and build them himself, without charge, but he was able to get materials at cost.

Now, therefore, I was able to lead the inspector into neat and professional-looking offices with rows of files in business-like order. All was not in order, however, at the farm. We were still using this house as a kind of emergency quarters, a place where kids could stay when there was no room at our place, while Geert and I got to know them and searched for suitable families. We did not have, the woman informed us, adequate toilet facilities for the number of children who were there at the moment. We tried to explain that the farm was a temporary expedient only: soon we hoped to have enough foster homes available that it would not be needed. She wasn't buying.

But the crushing blow came when she interviewed Geert and announced that the training he had received in Holland did not qualify him to be a children's counselor in the state of Pennsylvania. She pointed out that some of these children have emotional problems and that state law requires counselors to have a background in psychology. I knew it would be useless to point out to the woman that many people have emotional problems because they also have spiritual problems, and that any shortcomings Geert might have in his education were more than overcome by his sensitivity to the Lord's wisdom.

Overnight, we lost a large number of boys and girls on technical grounds—although some of the families were later able to reapply for these kids on the basis of the regular foster-home program. We decided to give up the farm at once, rather than spend a lot on new plumbing for a place we didn't intend to be using long. Besides, who knew whether we'd ever need that much space again? The Taylors stayed on to run the farm for the doctors who owned it; they are still our most faithful prayer supporters.

On top of our other losses, the home situations for both Joey and Jim had improved to the point where Geert agreed with the county caseworkers that the boys could return to their families. We were glad for their sakes, though the house was going to be awfully quiet. So the kids in the Bair household were reduced to the original cast—Ted, Marty, Judy, Jeanne, and Joni. It was very peaceful around the place and I was very depressed.

One night Marilyn said to me, "Bill, I've got two suggestions. First, I think you ought to go away for a few days—the change would do you good."

"Where could I go?"

"Why not go to Florida and attend the Holy Spirit Teaching Mission. And take Geert with you. You've both been down in the dumps lately and I think you need a new inspiration."

"I'll talk to Geert about it," I said. "What's your second suggestion?"

"It's selfish," she said. "Let's not take anybody else into the house right now. This has been a rough year on me. I've loved it, but I'm tired. I'd like us to be just by ourselves for a while."

"Looks like we're not going to have any choice about that, anyway," I said. "Okay, honey. You get a rest."

Geert liked Marilyn's idea and we left for Florida in the morning. Once again, Marilyn had been right. After a few days in Florida, Geert and I found ourselves getting excited again about the foundation. We realized that the shock of what had happened had momentarily turned our minds from the Lord. We agreed that God had led us into this work and that if He wanted us to stay in it He would provide the way. At the end of a week I telephoned Marilyn to tell her we were starting home.

"Then I'll see you tomorrow night?" she asked.

"That's right, honey."

"Bill. . . ." She hesitated.

"Yes, Marilyn?"

"Bill, I've got people here."

"You've got company?"

"Not really." She hesitated again. Then: "Well, I might as well tell you so you can laugh yourself out before you get back. Yesterday I got a call from a young widow who's been working, trying to raise five children. She'd fallen behind in her rent, Bill, and was about to be evicted. She asked me if I knew a place they could stay for a while."

I put in, "So now they're all living on the third floor of our house."

"Yes."

I laughed. "I'm glad you had such a nice, long rest."

"I had to, Bill," she said. "They had no place to go. Besides, it's too quiet around here these days."

"Marilyn," I said, "I love you."

# 10

Geert and I went back to work, counseling the remaining kids in our various love homes, processing new applications, traveling to Pittsburgh to try to pick up the pieces of our legal situation. As the weeks passed, we began to discover that we had friends everywhere. Judges, lawyers, probation officers, caseworkers, institutional supervisors—all not only agreed, but absolutely insisted that we be allowed to continue receiving both welfare and court-awarded children. These professionals had seen with their own eyes what could happen to a young person after only a few months in the kind of environment our families provided, and they weren't about to let a resource like this be taken from them.

Before long, we were receiving more children than we ever had, as the foundation suddenly seemed known all over the state. Not only courts and welfare agencies but public-supported orphanages began coming to us with children they felt could be helped more in a home situation. Looking back over our recent anxiety and discouragement, we saw what we should have seen all along: God's hand, sure and unerring in every detail. The mistake in bypassing the regional office had simply been a case of our stupidity working to His glory. If an inspector had come to visit us in the beginning, as should have happened—I shivered all over to think of it. What did we have then but an abandoned farmhouse and some vague ideas?

Now we had experience behind us, we had grasped God's plan of placing children with Christian families, we could argue for our approach by pointing to results. Above all, we were that all-important thing in the world of officials: an established fact. It was the only way a guy like me could ever have gotten started—through some kind of accident—and all I could do was praise God that I was accident-prone.

Geert Steenwyk and I began now, too, to spend more time with the families, both the families that wanted to start love homes and the families from which the troubled young people came. The best place for any child, we both agreed, is with his natural parents. When, for any reason, the parents cannot cope with themselves or with each other, the child may be better off for a while somewhere else. But Geert felt that this should be a temporary situation and that everybody involved should know it from the beginning. Trying to consider the needs of the child and his family, and of the foster family, we worked out the system we found most effective—although circumstances do not always allow the complete procedure in every case.

Usually we meet the child first, often in a caseworker's office, sometimes at the child's home, occasionally in a correctional institution or in jail. We try to have two of us from the foundation there at that initial meeting, partly so we'll have two opinions later when the board sits down to discuss what we can do for this child, but also because with two people it's easier to keep a conversation going with a young person who is frightened or hostile.

If we don't meet the child with his parents, we call on them next, again two of us. As we tell the parents about the foundation, we assure them that we realize we will have the child with us only temporarily, until the circumstances that require this separation are cleared up. The trouble may be death, illness, or some other situation over which the family has no control. Other times, however, there are things the natural parents can do to improve the home setup, and it's astonishing how often a few sessions with Geert lead to real change.

The child then moves in with Marilyn, the kids, and me for anywhere from a few weeks to a few months, finding out what life is like in a Christian, Spirit-filled household. During this period, we try to decide on the right foster family for him. Over the first five years of the foundation's existence, we acquired seventy-five love homes in the western Pennsylvania area alone, from which to choose. In the beginning, most of these families were our friends, many of them on our board of directors. Then others began to hear about us and come or write asking to have a part in this work. Again, two of us make the home investigation. We watch how the family relate to one another. If there are children, we especially want to know how they feel about having a stranger in the home. We talk to the neighbors, the father's employer, the family's pastor. As Geert says, "Never put a troubled child into a troubled home."

We have found that some foster parents are more effective

with younger teen-agers, while others work better with older ones. Some families do better with boys, others with girls. We have a middle-aged Catholic couple, who never had children of their own, who have turned out to be remarkably effective with retarded children, not only having the extra love these kids need, but time to give them special training. Some of our black foster families like to get black kids; other families enjoy a mixture of races.

When we feel we have found the right home for the child, we tell him all about it so that he has some idea of what to expect. We let him know that he doesn't have to go to this particular home and that if he finds out later he doesn't like it, he doesn't have to stay. Then we tell the foster parents all about the boy or girl we have for them, and try to iron out potential friction areas in advance. If it's a Catholic child, for example, and the family is Protestant, we make sure they can arrange to get him to mass. Or if the kid's bringing an amplified guitar, we find out how far his room will be from the parlor, and how strong the family's eardrums are.

Only then do we arrange the first meeting. We try to schedule it for a time when all of the foster family will be at home and the foster mother can serve a snack. This helps keep a light and general conversation going. Later, and separately, we find out how both the family and the child have reacted. In almost every case, everyone wants to give the thing a chance.

For the first two or three weeks of the new arrangement, both the young person and the foster family are on their best behavior, seeking to please. But people can put on this act just so long, then they have to relax and become themselves. This is when unexpected and unpleasant traits appear, in the family, in the child, or both. Therefore—it happens so often we've come to expect it—the boy or girl runs away from the foster home anywhere from four to six weeks after entering it. So far, we haven't lost a child for more than a couple of days. Knowing him pretty well by this time, we have a fairly good idea of where he will head, most often toward his natural home.

After we locate him, Geert has a long talk with him to find out what went wrong. Then he talks to the family for their version. In most cases, with the party over, the child thinks he is being disciplined too much, maybe being required to go to church too much, or not being allowed to go to the movies often enough. Also in most cases, both the child and the family want to give the relationship a second chance. After this episode, the parents seldom have any more problems with their foster child than they do with their own.

When a problem with drugs or sex or dishonesty outwits the best efforts of the foster family, the whole foundation swings into action. Even when things are going smoothly we schedule regular weekly meetings and prayer times between each family and the foundation staff—and a weekly "family reunion" of all the households in an area. These are great times for swapping joys, hopes, and hard-won wisdom, among adults and kids alike.

But it's when things go wrong that the sense of belonging to a group—of being not just one small family battling its problems alone, but an organic part of a praying, believing, supporting body—becomes most crucial.

And it's during these times that all of us learn the most.

I remember one set of foster parents who brought to the gathered foundation family the problem of a new daughter who had been picked up three times by the New Wilmington police for shoplifting. Her compulsion to steal was turning out to be a genuine kleptomania which no amount of love, reassurance, and discipline was able to change. As the parents were pouring out their despair, another foster mother interrupted.

This lady and her husband had taken in a fifteen-year-old boy who was mainlining heroin when he first came to the foundation. He had seemed to experience a complete withdrawal as a result of some prayer sessions while in our house, but a few weeks after moving to his foster home, the familiar symptoms reappeared. "That was when I started doing some reading on the subject," the foster mother said. "And from what I read, once you started mainlining, you were finished. I think I really stopped believing then that he could change. Oh, I kept on praying. You know the kind of thing: 'God, You can do anything. You can heal him.'

"And then one night when I was going on this way, God said to me, *Yes. I can. I can heal Henry. But do you believe I* will *heal him?*

"Well, I got to thinking about that and I thought, Yes of course God will heal him! Since He loves him, and He *can* do it, He *will* do it! From then on I just praised God that He was going to do this—and inside the month Henry was off heroin for good."

She turned to the other pair: "I think you're letting the word 'kleptomania' come between you and God. You're saying, 'She's a kleptomaniac,' instead of looking to see what God will do."

Well, then and there the whole roomful of us got down on our knees and just thanked and praised God for the difference between *can* and *will,* and that He was going to heal this girl completely. God did heal her, and today she holds a responsible job in—of all places—a large department store in downtown Philadelphia.

So important is such prayer backup to the work of the foundation that we now have a special "prayer corps" which devotes full time to this job. These are often elderly people or invalids who cannot take a child physically into their homes, but can take him into their hearts and hold him up to God hour after hour, while the foster mother may be so deep in dishwater and missing shirt buttons that she has time only for an occasional "Help, Lord!"

It was Dr. Ada Peabody, a retired music professor from Westminster College, who gave the name "fanner bees" to these prayer workers. In the beehive, she explains, certain individuals, instead of flying out on various errands, remain at their stations moving their wings to bring a constant flow of life-giving air into the nest. In our case it is the breath of the Spirit on which every other phase of the work depends; and over seventy fanner bees take on this work of intercession twenty-four hours a day, every day in the year.

This kind of power is bound to show. Of the more than three hundred children who came to us during our first five years, about 80 percent made commitments to Jesus Christ, and about half of these experienced the Baptism in the Holy Spirit. For ourselves, it's this sense of being held up on a river of prayer and praise that gives us courage in situations where human wisdom isn't enough—and for me that's any-time. What Geert said his very first day turned out to be uncomfortably true: there's no textbook approach to a kid. Each one is different, each one is special, each one requires God Almighty to understand him.

I remember one Christmas in particular that was like a miniature of the whole work of the foundation. Geert had asked permission to fly to Holland to spend the holidays with his family.

We had only four kids in the house besides our own, just then, fewer than usual because we'd tried to get everyone settled with his "permanent" foster family for Christmas. These four, however, had just come.

Shirley was from out of state. On a trip north the previous summer, I had given a speech at a local chapter of the Full Gospel Businessmen's Association, and, though I didn't know it at the time, Shirley's father was in the audience. He telephoned me the first week in December and asked if I could help his daughter. Shirley had dropped out of school and was running around with a motorbike gang. Most nights the gang and their girls slept on the floor in an abandoned basement, using drugs, having sex like animals. Time and again, her parents had gone to the basement and dragged Shirley out, but she always went back. Then her father remembered my talk about what we were achieving in our love homes with the help of the Holy Spirit.

I told him our decisions were made only after prayer by the whole staff, and I'd call him back the next day. I never got a chance to. Next morning, as we were having break-fast, a car pulled into the driveway. As the occupants got out, I knew it had to be Shirley and her parents. The girl had steel-rimmed glasses and long, blonde, very dirty hair. Her complexion was awful. Beneath a filthy, ankle-length coat I saw soiled jeans and torn sneakers. Her father had said she was seventeen but she was a tall girl, badly overweight, and I would have guessed she was a lot older. I didn't wait for the three of them to knock, but opened the door as they were coming up the steps and greeted them by name. Inside, I introduced them to Marilyn and the kids, and Marilyn offered them breakfast. Shirley's father said they had stopped for breakfast on the road but that he, at least, could do with some coffee. Marilyn began to prepare three cups, but Shirley said, "I don't want anything."

My daughter Joni said, "Shirley, I'd love to have you share my room! Come on upstairs. I'll show you where it is."

Not only was this typical ministering by one of our kids, but it was good timing, giving us a chance to discuss Shirley without her sitting there. Her parents could not understand why she had changed so much over the past year. Until then, she had been sweet, cheery, bright, studious. Then she just seemed to let go of everything, neglecting herself, staying out late, sometimes not coming home at all. One night, the parents were awakened by a roar of motorcycles outside their home; they got to the window in time to see Shirley coming up the walk as the pack roared off. Glad to have her home under any circumstances, they asked no questions.

This fall, after only a few weeks of school, Shirley had dropped out. This was when she started staying away from home for three or four days at a time. One night at the gang's headquarters Shirley became ill, perhaps from drugs, and telephoned her father to come and get her. This was how the man found out about the snake pit in the basement. After that, whenever Shirley stayed away from home more than one night, he went to the basement and literally dragged her out. The rest of the gang was usually asleep or too drugged to give him any resistance; besides, they were confident she'd be back.

Joni and Shirley had been upstairs about fifteen minutes when Joni came down and said, "I don't want to be a tattle-tale, Dad, but Shirley is smoking upstairs, and it doesn't smell like tobacco."

I turned to Shirley's parents: "Did you know that Shirley smokes marijuana?"

"Yes."

"And you don't try to stop her?"

"She says it's no more harmful than ordinary tobacco."

"Something's harming her, though, from what you say—harming her a lot." I prayed silently for a moment, then suggested, "I think maybe it would be easier for Shirley, easier for you too, if you just left now, without saying good-bye."

I waited until the car was out of the driveway. Then I went upstairs to Shirley. She was sitting on a bed, hunched over, the joint in one hand, using the other hand as an ashtray. Entering, I said, "Shirley, put that thing out." As I went to her, she exhaled a cloud of pungent smoke. "Come on, Shirley, put it out."

Without looking at me she said, "There's no ashtray."

"We don't have ashtrays," I said. "Nobody smokes around here." I waited a moment, and when she did not move I reached out and took the butt from her. Wetting a couple of fingers, I pinched the cigarette out, crumpled it, and dropped it in a wastebasket. Her shoulder bag was next to her. I said, "Open your bag. I want the rest of those things."

She said, "No. I've got personal things in my bag. You have no right."

I said, "I'm not interested in your personal things. But this is my house and I don't allow marijuana in it. Open your bag."

When she still didn't move, I picked up the bag. Instantly she was on her feet, snatching at the purse, trying to get it away from me. I grabbed her wrist and gave it a sharp squeeze. She let out a scream and threw herself on the bed in tears, acting more hurt than she could possibly have been. I let her play out her scene for a few moments, and then I said, "Shirley, as a member of this family, you will have your rights. But the possession of marijuana is illegal in this state, and I have the right to prevent a crime from being committed in my own home. Will you open this bag and give me the marijuana, or do I have to look for it myself?"

She got up, the sobbing over, and took the bag from me. Opening it, she fished around and brought up four more sticks of marijuana. "That's all I have," she said.

"I'll take your word for it," I said, holding out my hand for them.

She closed her fist around them. "I won't smoke them around the house." It was almost a plea.

"You're not going to smoke them at all," I said. I reached for her wrist and squeezed again. She opened her fist and I took the cigarettes. "Now, Shirley, why don't you take off your coat and hang it in the closet and come on downstairs and join the family?"

"I don't feel like it."

"All right," I said. "Whenever you feel like it, just come down." I went into the bathroom, tore the cigarettes to shreds, and flushed them. In the kitchen my four daughters were helping Marilyn clean up after breakfast. "You gals have got your work cut out for you this time," I said, and they all rolled their eyes.

The second child to enter our home that December was Jeff, age fifteen. In this case, too, fairly untypically, it was the parents who had contacted us, saying they could no longer control their son. Jeff had started running around with a rough crowd and was having some close calls with the police, such as driving around in a car which he said he didn't know was stolen, acting as lookout during some shoplifting in department stores, throwing rocks at school windows. Geert had already left for Holland, so I went alone the next day to meet the family. They had a nice home in a good neighborhood. I noticed two cars in the garage, plus an expensive bicycle. The house was attractively and expensively furnished. We rarely got kids from a background like this. Jeff was an only child. His parents had married young and were still in their mid-thirties. Both worked; the father was a real estate and insurance salesman, the mother an interior decorator. Both had to see their customers at the customer's convenience, which often meant evening appointments, frequently with both of them out of the house. In a way, this explained the family's affluence; in another way it also explained the family's problem.

After I had visited with Jeff and his parents for about twenty minutes, I looked at the boy, seated on a sofa across the room, and said, "Jeff, let's get to why I am here. You have a nice home. Your parents seem to be fine people. They're really concerned about you—I can see that. Why do you think you've been getting yourself into trouble lately?"

Jeff looked right at me. "There's nothing to do around here. Nobody pays any attention to me."

"You know that's not true, Jeff," his father said hotly. "Tell us the last time your mother and I denied you anything. Tell us the last time we refused to let you do something you wanted to do." He stood up. "Mr. Bair, I want to show you something."

We all went down to the basement. It looked like a sporting goods catalog. Just about every kind of hobby material, sports equipment, or game that would interest a teen-age boy was hanging from the ceiling, lined along the walls, or strewn on tabletops. The only thing missing was an indoor swimming pool.

The father said, "How about this, Mr. Bair? Does this look like he has nothing to do around here?"

I said, "Gosh, Jeff, this is terrific. I know lots of kids who would give their right arm for half of this."

Jeff said, "Let me tell you something you won't find down here, Mr. Bair. You won't find it anywhere in this whole house."

I could see that the boy was really uptight. "What's that, Jeff?"

"Love."

"Oh, Jeff," I said, trying to cover up his parents' shock and embarrassment, "there's love in this house. I can feel it. Your folks love you."

His mother said softly, hurt, "Of course we love you."

He looked at her. "Then why won't you give me some of your time?"

This was a stopper. I'd come upon many situations in which this was the family problem—parents with no time for their children—but this was the first time I'd heard the child lay it on the line quite like that. Most often, the child feels neglected without identifying the cause, certainly not verbalizing it.

There was a silence. I said, "Well, Jeff, that's why I'm here. Let's go upstairs and talk about it."

Upstairs, I made a point of joining Jeff on the sofa. His mother made coffee. As we continued talking, I casually stretched out my arm along the back of the sofa, positioning my hand so that, when I wanted to bring Jeff into the conversation, I could touch his shoulder. He became aware of this at once but did not move; I wondered how long it had been since his father touched him with any affection. We talked for about an hour more, and then the time came for Jeff to make his decision.

I said, "You can come home with me now, Jeff, or you can wait until after Christmas."

"I'll go now," he said.

"You won't be able to come home for Christmas," I pointed out.

"Christmas is no good around here anyway," he said. "I'll go pack." He went upstairs to his room.

I said to his parents, "I know this must hurt you very much."

"It hurts like crazy," the father said.

Jeff's mother said, "I had no idea he hated us so."

"He doesn't hate you," I said. "He's just feeling rejected and he's trying to strike back. After Jeff gets settled with us, you'll be able to visit him and bring him home for weekends. I suggest you try not to have business appointments during those weekends. A man from the foundation, Geert Steenwyk, will be getting in touch with you; he's very wise about these things. And don't worry about Jeff. He loves you. If he didn't, he wouldn't care that you don't have time for him, as he seems to think."

Jeff came down with his suitcase. He kissed his mother good-bye, but just nodded at his father. We left at once. The hasty departure turned out to be a good idea: Jeff was so choked up that he couldn't speak for the first half hour. Maybe he thought he was punishing his parents by leaving them, but he wasn't enjoying the experience so much him-self. Kids never do.

Finally he asked, "Mr. Bair, you really like people, don't you?"

"I love people, Jeff," I replied.

"Yeah," he said, nodding thoughtfully. "I could tell."

When we got home, Ted was there. Ted was now study-ing electrical engineering at a technical school in Pittsburgh; he was nineteen, a tall, terrific-looking young man. All of our kids had become so zealous in their ministry to the foundation's children that a newcomer was like live bait. Ted almost broke Jeff's arm with his handshake. "I'll put your suitcase in our room, Jeff," he said.

Jeff said, "Our room?"

"It'll be mostly yours," Ted said. "I'm just here on week-ends and holidays. But I'd like you to use it and maybe you won't mind dusting off my guns every few days."

"You got guns?"

"Yeah. Do you? Do you like to hunt?"

"I've got guns," Jeff said, "but nobody ever took me hunt-ing yet."

"Maybe we can get some hunting in over the holidays,"

Ted said. "Come on, I'll show you my guns." As they scampered up the stairs, I was sure I wouldn't have any trouble with Jeff as long as Ted was around.

The third child we had in the house that Christmas was Barbara, sixteen, from New Jersey. Leonard Evans had called me about her. Her parents had been members of his church before they moved to the States—as had Barbara herself. But down in New Jersey the girl had gotten involved in witchcraft—complete with Ouija boards, card reading, crystal balls, hypnotism. There followed long periods of depression, and several suicide attempts. She had been placed in two different mental institutions, but released when nobody could figure out what was wrong with her.

I said, "Leonard, you know I'd never say no to you, but if this girl is a mental case we certainly can't help her."

"If it was mental illness, wouldn't all those doctors have spotted it?" he asked. "I'm sure it's something else, Bill, and the Lord has given me the feeling that you can help her. Will you take her, Bill?"

"I can't refuse, Leonard. But you'll have to agree that we can send her back if we realize we can't handle her."

"I'll agree to that," he said. "Bill, I've already checked on planes. We can have Barbara in Pittsburgh around five this afternoon. Geert knows her, from our church. Can he meet her?"

"Geert's in Holland for the holidays."

"I didn't know that."

"What does she look like? I'll meet her."

"Well, Bill," he said, "just look for a girl who doesn't have a face."

"No face?"

"It's her hair. Dark brown. She wears it down to her waist, but like an umbrella. It goes clear around."

I had no trouble recognizing Barbara at the airport: I had to look at her feet to find out which way she was facing so that I could approach her from the right direction. She had nothing to say for herself as we drove back to New Wilmington, and after awhile I got tired of doing all the talking. After twenty minutes of dead silence she asked me if I was a doctor, and I told her I wasn't. Silence the rest of the way. We got home just in time to have supper with the family, now including Shirley and Jeff, and the only times anybody got a glimpse of Barbara's face were when she pulled her hair aside to put some food into her mouth. If it weren't for the fact that we knew this was a very troubled girl, the situation would have been almost funny. After supper, she said she was tired and wanted to lie down. We put her in Marty and Jeanne's room.

It was around half-past nine when Jeanne came to me and said, "Dad, Barbara and Shirley have their heads together in our room."

This was not good. "Kids with similar problems have a way of smelling each other out," Geert liked to say. "If they ever make a real partnership it will be twice as hard to help either one, because they won't really have changed their environment." It had happened before in our house. It had also happened that a newcomer to the foundation without an acquaintance for miles around would find local kids with his identical hang-ups on his first stroll—and New Wilmington is a small town.

Jeff was passing through the room. "Jeff," I said, "please

go upstairs and tell Shirley and Barbara that we'll be starting prayers in a few minutes."

He glanced at his watch. "Already?"

"Yes. I feel like singing a lot of hymns tonight."

In a few minutes the whole family was gathered in the living room, Marilyn at the organ, and I saw to it that Shirley and Barbara sat as far apart as possible. We went on for over an hour. Then we formed a circle and joined hands to pray together. To my surprise, sounds that certainly weren't English began to emanate from the thicket of hair hiding Barbara's face. Leonard Evans had said nothing about her receiving the Baptism of the Spirit, and somehow the noises she was making didn't sound like prayer. I was puzzled by it.

We all went to bed. Around midnight, Marty burst into our room, waking Marilyn and me: "Barbara has locked herself in the bathroom! She said she's going to slash her wrists."

The shock froze me for a moment. "You say the door is locked?"

"Yes, Dad."

I jumped out of bed. "Wake up Ted."

Marilyn asked, "Is there anything in there she can use?"

"My razor blades, for one thing."

The bathroom light showed under the door. I tried the knob. "Barbara, open the door."

"No," came her voice from inside. "I'm going to kill myself."

I said, "Barbara, open the door this minute. I'm getting mad."

"I don't care. I'm going to kill myself."

Ted arrived. I told him, "We're going to have to break it down." We banged our shoulders against the door three or four times before the lock snapped and the door swung open. Barbara was at the sink, her back to us. I swung her around. She held a blade in her right hand and on the underside of her left wrist she had made a small cut, well to the side of the vein. I prayed for self-control and the right words. I took the blade away from her and threw it into the wastebasket. I got the adhesive tape from the medicine cabinet and applied an inch of it to the cut. Then I said, "Now, you go back to your bed. And if you set foot out of it before morning, you'll be confined to the house for a week." The noise had awakened the other kids on the second floor, and I sent them all back to bed. Then I retrieved the blade from the wastebasket and took my other blades and the scissors and anything else Barbara might use if she decided to try this again, and headed back to the bedroom.

Marilyn was standing in the doorway. "Was it a bad cut?"

"No. She didn't mean it. People who are always threatening suicide never go through with it." But I didn't feel as sure as I tried to sound.

Barbara did not come down for breakfast, and this gave me a chance to discuss the whole event with the rest of the family. I told the kids not to mention the suicide attempt to Barbara. If she ever threatened suicide again they were not to get excited, but just to let me know. I also asked for their prayers that the Lord would show me how I could help Barbara.

After breakfast I went upstairs. Barbara was up and dressed, sitting on a chair, head bowed, her face, as always, hidden by her hair. Though I tried for half an hour, I couldn't get a word out of her. At last I gave up trying to get information out of her and just talked to her about Jesus, assuring her that there wasn't a problem in the world that He couldn't solve if only she would ask Him. I noticed something peculiar. Every time I said the name "Jesus," a shudder seemed to pass through Barbara, as though a chill had struck. I couldn't figure it out. Finally I left her alone.

Ten minutes later, Ted came running into my office hollering, "Dad! Dad! Barbara's in the kitchen and she's got a carving knife!"

The two of us hurried into the house. Barbara was at the sink, the big knife in her hand. Across the room were Jeff and Jeanne, their faces full of terror. I walked to Barbara and grabbed the knife away from her.

Then, pulling back her hair, I slapped her. I said, "That's for interrupting me at my work." I slapped her again. "That's for scaring the kids." A third time: "And that's for disobeying me. I told you I didn't want you to try this again, and as long as you're under my roof I expect you to obey me." I handed the knife to Ted for safekeeping and went back to my office.

Barbara was not at the lunch table. I was surprised that she was still in the house.

After lunch, I spent a couple of hours driving around visiting our love homes. Nothing made me feel better than visiting a house where one of our kids was coming along well, and I was very much in need of some good feelings. These kids always made me remember how strung out they had been when we first got them. Their lives and their relationships had been a mess; now after only a few months of solid loving from their new family, we generally had a new person on our hands, a kid who was going to make it.

Not always, of course. We'd had failures before, and al-

ways because it turned out that the child had some problem—usually a sex problem—that nobody knew about when
he or she was sent to us. Not that sexual problems in themselves were any harder for the Lord to handle than any
other human weakness. We'd had them all, at one time or
another, in our house: homosexuality, child molesting, ani-
mal contact—and we'd seen these aberrations vanish like
dew on a sunny morning when God's healing love shone on
them.

Our failures came when we were unaware of the problem
until some misadventure made it public knowledge and a
scandal in our little town. Even so, we had still been able
to help some of these children by moving them to different
localities, starting anew, knowing now what to watch for,
how to protect them and those around them, how to pray.
Three we had to surrender to the police or an institution.
And in each case we felt the fault was ours, not the child's,
because we had not sought and prayed enough.

But this day was different; Christmas was in the air. All
the foster kids I visited were adjusting terrifically; at each
house we played the guess-what-I'm-giving-you game. I saw
such joy and love in these homes that I just kept praising the
Lord for letting me be part of all this. There were actually
moments when I did not think of Barbara at all.

As soon as I got home, I sensed something was wrong.
The house was too quiet. I found Marilyn standing at the
foot of the stairs, and I could see she had been crying. "It's
Barbara," she said. "She has Ted's hunting knife. She's up
on the third floor. I've been up there a dozen times, but
she won't even speak to me."

I shook my head. "I wish I knew what to do," I said. I

went up to the third floor, slowly, bewildered, praying. She was sitting on a cot, looking down at the knife which she held to her wrist, her hair hiding her face. I knew how sharp that knife was and realized she could cut herself badly even if she didn't intend to. I stood there watching her for a minute or two. Then I said, "Go ahead, Barbara." She didn't move. I said, "Why don't you get it over with, Barbara? This whole thing is getting a little boring."

"I want to die," she said, not moving.

"Well, nobody around here is going to help you do it," I said. "You'll have to do it yourself. So please go ahead and do it now so that you don't ruin everybody's Christmas."

"What do you mean?" The voice behind the hair was indignant.

I said, "Well, Christmas is supposed to be a happy time, and it's just a few days off. Everybody here loves you, Barbara, and if you kill yourself we'll all feel bad. But since you seem determined to do it, please do it right away. Then we'll have time to ship your body back to New Jersey and get used to the idea that you're gone, before Christmas. Now, Barbara, that knife is sharp enough to cut your hand off without any trouble, so you can get it over quick. I promise I won't try to stop you."

For once I was glad of the great screen of hair; she couldn't see how I was trembling. Suddenly she threw back her head, her hair falling aside. I had never seen such anguish on a face. "I can't!" she screamed. The knife dropped to the floor. She sprang up and came toward me; I had no idea what to expect. Then she threw her arms around my neck and pressed her face against my chest and began to sob.

"What's the matter, Barbara?" I said. "What's troubling you, honey? No matter what it is, Barbara, the Lord can help you. Ask Jesus to help with it. No matter what the problem is, He can take it right out of your life. Let's pray together now and ask Jesus to help."

"I can't, I can't," she kept saying, "I can't. Don't ask me to do that. I can't. I can't do it."

She was shaking all over. I had no idea whether anything had been achieved or not.

The fourth newcomer to our house was Herbert, thirteen, from a neighboring county. Herbert's father was a heavy drinker who, when he got drunk enough, would start beating up the family. Also, the man owned a revolver, and it was not unusual for him, when drinking, to start shooting. Two weeks before Christmas the man had come home drunk and started on Herbert's mother. Herbert went and got the revolver and fired a warning shot over his father's head. The noise sobered the man immediately. Herbert surrendered the gun and accepted a few clouts on the ears. Then his father telephoned the police to say that his son had just shot at him and that he wanted to have the boy taken away.

I heard about Herbert through his district juvenile officer. He was a pretty sad sight when I arrived to pick him up. I found him sitting in the officer's room weeping noiselessly, his cap and overcoat on, his suitcase in front of him. I never saw such big tears come out of a kid. They were the size of marbles as they rolled down his cheeks, and where they hit his coat they made blotches the size of quarters. I talked to him about the foundation, but he gave no sign that I was getting through to him. When I suggested that we head home, however, he stood up, picked up his suitcase, and came along without any resistance. All the way home, the tears kept flowing.

At home, I helped him out of his hat and coat, then introduced him to the people who were there. As he went around the room shaking hands, the big tears continued to flow. I asked Ted to help Herbert get settled up on the third floor. When Ted came back to the living room, Joni asked, "Is he still crying?"

Ted said, "Yes. Dad, does he always do that?"

"Ever since I've seen him," I said.

We sat around waiting for Herbert to come down. When he didn't appear after twenty minutes I asked Jeff to go up and get him. Jeff came back quickly. "He's not up there."

"He isn't?"

"I looked all around."

"Did you try on the second floor?"

"No."

"Would you do that, please?"

Jeff took the stairs three at a time but returned shaking his head. "He's not there, either."

Judy spoke what we were all thinking: "I wonder if he went out the back way and ran away?"

"I hope not," said Marilyn. "Here's his cap and overcoat."

I said, "Let's all look."

We spread out all over the house, calling Herbert's name. I had just decided that I'd better get out the car when somebody noticed that Ted was missing, too. I went back up to the third floor once more. "Ted? Herbert? Are you up here?"

Ted's voice answered, "We're over here, Dad."

I couldn't see anyone. "Where?"

"Under the bed."

I dropped to my knees and looked. There was Ted with an arm around Herbert's shoulders. I asked, "What are you doing under the bed?"

Ted said, "I was just telling Herbert about all the fun we have in this house."

So Ted had found him there and, when he wouldn't come out, had crawled in with him. "Okay. But bring him down in a little while. The rest of us want to get to know him, too." I went downstairs with the good news.

About fifteen minutes later, Ted and Herbert appeared, Ted in his ski cap and heavy jacket. "Herbert and I are going bobsledding," he said. "Anyone want to come along?"

Most of the kids went, and I knew that they would see to it that Herbert got most of the rides. When they came back in a couple of hours, they were all laughing and talking at once. Herbert, his cheeks flushed, his eyes no longer streaming, looked like a different boy.

We also seemed to be making progress with Shirley. The week before, during our weekly half hour alone with Marty, she had said suddenly, "Dad and Mom, I think I know what's troubling Shirley. I think she feels she's not good looking."

We asked her what made her think that. Marty said, "Mom, how many times have you seen a girl pass a mirror without looking at herself in it?"

Marilyn said, "I don't know. I've never thought of it."

Marty asked, "Don't you look at yourself?"

"I don't know," Marilyn said. "I suppose I do check my hair and my makeup."

"Right," Marty said. "Most girls do. But Shirley doesn't. I've watched her. She doesn't even look into a mirror while she's brushing her teeth. And she doesn't fuss with her hair the way the rest of us do. She's the same way about her clothes. She just doesn't care; she's given up on herself. She *is* tall, you know, and she's overweight and she has all those pimples. Maybe I shouldn't say this, but I wouldn't be surprised if the reason Shirley joined that motorcycle gang was that she thought it was the only way she could get attention from a boy."

I said, "Couldn't you tell her that Jesus Christ loves people no matter what they look like?"

Marty frowned at me. "Dad, how could I say a thing like that to Shirley without hurting her?"

"Then we'll have to trick her," I said. "Marilyn, are you going to the beauty parlor before Christmas?"

"The day after tomorrow."

"Why don't you take Shirley along?" I suggested. "Just say you want some company. Once you get her in there, maybe she'll let them do something with her hair."

"It's worth a try."

Marty said, "Dad, remember a few years ago, when Judy's face started breaking out? You got something from the doctor."

I remembered. "I'll call the doctor when I get back to the office. Marilyn, what chores does Shirley have around the house?"

"She helps with the dishes after meals."

"Why don't you give her some jobs that require more walking, like dusting or running the vacuum?"

Marilyn shook her head. "I don't think that will help much."

"Maybe we could get her to jog with Ted in the mornings," said Marty.

"But after Christmas Ted will be going back to school," said Marilyn.

"We'll start the Bair Jogging Club," Marty said. "I'll join, too. The only problem will be to keep it going once Ted leaves."

"You get her started and she'll want to keep going," I prophesied. "One more thing. I think we should start singing 'Jesus Loves Me' a lot more around here."

The following week, in fact the very day Herbert arrived, I had two telephone calls within an hour of each other, one from Shirley's parents, one from Barbara's, both families asking if the girls could come home for Christmas. I explained the foundation's policy of keeping a child with us a couple of months at least before his first visit to his old environment. Although Shirley and Barbara were special cases, because they had not come to us through the usual channels, there were, I said, two boys in the house who would have to follow the rule, and I felt it was only fair for Shirley and Barbara to follow it also. But I invited the families to come to New Wilmington the week after Christmas and spend a few days with us. Both pairs of parents jumped at the suggestion.

I told Marilyn about this, but not the girls, deciding that the news would make a nice present on Christmas Day. Marilyn was counting on her fingers. "Fifteen people," she said. "And December's a hard month on the household account."

"The Lord will provide," I said airily.

"He'd better," she said.

A few days after Barbara broke down and sobbed in my arms, there was a showing on television of Dickens's *A Christmas Carol*. Over supper, the whole family agreed to watch it together. There had been no dramatic change in Barbara following her outburst. She still had very little to say for herself, but at least she showed up for meals, and under the urging of the Bair girls was wearing her hair pulled at least part way back, to reveal a thin, dark-eyed face that would have been beautiful if it had not been so sad.

Before the television show, the kids had lined up the chairs in the living room like a movie theater. The girls had made a big batch of popcorn and the boys and I had driven to the store for some six-packs of soft drinks. We were all in our seats when the movie began. I noticed Barbara seated to one side by herself. The alliance I had feared between her and Shirley had not materialized. Shirley, I thought, looked better already: her long yellow hair was freshly shampooed and shining; she wore a pretty new blouse over the inevitable dungarees. But Barbara—those heartbroken eyes haunted me.

Then as I sat watching the familiar saga of the spirits of Christmas Past, Present, and Future, a thought struck me which turned my blood to ice. I had to give myself a couple of minutes before I could move. Then I got up and tiptoed around behind the sofa, where Marilyn and Herbert were sitting holding hands. I whispered in Marilyn's ear, "You know what Don Basham's special ministry is."

Her eyes on the TV set, she nodded. "Deliverance."

"Honey," I said, "I think we've got a young lady in this house who could use some of that."

Startled, she looked at me, then glanced around the room. "Barbara?"

"Yes. It just hit me. Don once told me that the one thing evil spirits can't stand is the name of Jesus. You know what Barbara goes through whenever she hears that word."

"Oh, Bill."

"I wish I could get Don Basham up here for a few days."

"Why don't you call him?"

"I couldn't ask him to leave his family at Christmas."

"Well, ask him to come after Christmas."

"I'll write him tomorrow." I went back to my chair.

Twenty minutes later the telephone rang. Jeanne went out to the kitchen to answer it. "It's for you, Dad," she called.

"Did you ask who it was?"

"It's long-distance. The operator asked for you."

I went out to the phone. "Bill Bair?" said the operator.

"Speaking."

"Go ahead, sir. Here's your party."

"Hi, Bill!" came a man's voice. "Merry Christmas to you and the family. It's Don Basham."

A few minutes ago, he said, he'd gotten a tremendous urge to see some snow again at Christmastime. What would we think if he and the family drove up after Christmas?

I practically floated back to the living room. "Who was that on the phone?" asked Marilyn, whispering so as not to interfere with Tiny Tim.

"Don Basham."

She beamed the smile of a believer who remains amazed by the ways of the Lord. "How fantastic! What did he want?"

"They're coming to visit us for a few days right after Christmas."

"How wonderful, Bill!" Then the smile wavered. "With the five children?"

"Of course."

She counted again. "That's twenty-two people. Bill, we're going to have twenty-two people to feed!"

"We've had more than that plenty of times."

"Not with the food budget overspent already."

"You're starting to sound like Scrooge," I reproached her. "The Lord's sending them, so the Lord will feed them." And I turned my attention back to the screen.

The morning of Christmas Eve began early at our house, with friends of the foundation arriving with gifts for the foster children in love homes throughout the area. As we catalogued the gifts, a second parade began, local women bringing in fruits and vegetables they had put up early in the fall, sacks of potatoes, pies, cakes, cookies. The kitchen began to look like a supermarket, complete with a huge turkey from a foundation director who raised them, and for once Marilyn had to confess that I'd been right.

After lunch, Jeff came over to me and said, "Dad, can I go home and spend Christmas with my parents?"

I said, "No, Jeff, I'm sorry. I told you that the day we met, remember? I was willing to let you stay home and come here after Christmas, but you wanted to come right away. Well, you know the rules." When he still looked unconvinced, I added, "I'll tell you a secret, but you've got to keep it a secret. The other day I had calls from both Shirley's and Barbara's parents, wanting the girls home for Christmas, and I told them no. But I did invite them here for a few days afterward. If you want, Jeff, I'll call your folks and ask them to come too."

He thought about it. "That's okay, I understand. Forget it."

And, like a dope, I forgot it.

The day flew past; the next thing I knew it was time for the Christmas Eve service at the church. The eleven of us walked there together. A light snow was falling on the old snow that crunched under our feet. I felt very happy, and grateful to the Lord for more reasons than I could count. Since there is nothing a person can do for God except love Him and obey Him, my Christmas prayer was that, through the Holy Spirit, I would always be sensitive to His will.

As we were coming out of church, we ran into the Hamners, one of our love families. With three daughters of their own, they preferred girls to boys from the foundation. Over the years, they had taken two and done excellent jobs with them. I introduced the newest arrivals to them, and noticed how they took to Barbara right away. The three Hamner girls gathered around her while Will and Ann Hamner kept glancing at her almost hungrily. As the family was walking home, Marilyn and I bringing up the rear, I asked, "Did you notice how the Hamners reacted to Barbara?"

"Yes. Love at first sight."

More and more often God seemed to be putting people together with this instant and mysterious affinity. "That may be where Barbara goes when she's ready."

At home, Marty and Ted kept us between tears and laughter with their account of their first Christmas with us. They told how they cried continually and no gifts pleased them and they screamed at each new sight and sound. I knew why they were doing this: they realized this Christmas Eve was tough on Shirley, Barbara, Jeff, and Herbert. It was the first time for any of them away from home. They wanted to show them they understood.

At bedtime we had just formed our circle for prayers when Marty said suddenly, "Dad, Shirley has a Christmas present for you."

I looked at Shirley in the dress she had put on for church, and which did so much more for her heavyset figure than the skintight jeans she generally wore. I don't know what kind of concoction she had on her face, but her complexion looked better too. "That's nice, honey," I said, "but save it for morning. We always exchange gifts on Christmas morning."

Shirley said, "I know, Dad, but this is something different. I'd like to give you this present now, so that I'll always remember when it happened. Dad, I want to commit my life to Jesus Christ this Christmas Eve."

Out of the corner of my eye I saw a little spasm of shaking seize Barbara. I asked, "Shirley, do you want to do this because it is in your heart or because you know it will make me happy?"

"I want to make you happy," she said, "but, even more, it's in my heart. I know it."

"Tell them about it," said Marty.

Shirley shrugged. "It's hard to put into words. I didn't like this place when I first got here. I thought you were all religious fanatics. I knew why my parents brought me here— to get me off drugs and away from my friends—and I hated them for it.

"But I guess I hated everything and everybody then. I wasn't ready for what I found here—people having so much fun, everybody always busy. Well, I don't know what happened. In the past few days, my whole life has changed. I'm taking an interest in things again. I'm my old self. Better than that, I'm somebody new. I can't explain it, but I've been thinking about it, and I figure it must be Jesus. So I told Marty today that I wanted to give my life to Him, and it was her idea that I should do it now, tonight, at prayers."

"It's the best Christmas present I ever got," I said. "Why don't you kneel in the middle of the circle, and we'll all pray for you as you make your commitment."

Shirley knelt, and then I heard, "I want to do it, too, Dad."

I looked at Herbert, astonished. "You, too?"

"Yes," he said. "Is it all right?"

"Of course, as long as it really is your own decision."

"It is."

"Then kneel with Shirley."

The rest of us closed the circle and held hands as Shirley and Herbert made their commitments. Afterward there was laughing and crying and everybody was hugging and kissing. I said to Shirley, "Now I've got a present for you. Your parents are coming to visit you right after Christmas." She threw her arms around me. I looked for Barbara to give her the same news. Only then did I notice that she was not in the room.

I found her upstairs in her bed, the light out, apparently asleep, although I doubted that. But since she was obviously not in the mood to talk, I went out again and the rest of us went to bed too.

It was half-past one when I was awakened by the sound of a car stopping in front of the house. In an instant I was on my feet, fears for Barbara filling my mind. But when I reached the window it was Jeff, not Barbara, whom I saw run quickly down the snowy walk and climb into the backseat of a car. Before I could get the window raised the car was gone.

I stood for a long time staring at where it had been, the December air chilling the room. It was no good setting out after someone who had a head start in an automobile, and yet I knew I was in some way responsible for what Jeff had just done. Something I had ·said. Something I hadn't said. Some way in which I'd let him down.

Next morning, our Christmas spirit was dampened somewhat by Jeff's absence. After breakfast, we exchanged our gifts, and the activity in itself made us feel a little better. We put Jeff's gifts aside. Then started the parade of visitors, including many foster parents and their families. It wasn't long before the house was filled with the fragrance of turkey, and we all made a big deal of just snacking at lunch to save our appetites for the big feast. I told Barbara that her folks were coming to see her, and was disturbed when she didn't show much reaction.

Around four, the phone rang and I heard, "Dad?"

"Who's this?"

"Jeff."

"Hello, Jeff."

"Dad, can I come home?"

"I never wanted you to leave."

"Then I can come home?"

"Certainly. Where are you? I'll pick you up."

"It's okay, Dad. I've got a lift. I'll be there in an hour and a half."

I went into the kitchen and took Marilyn aside. "How soon will dinner be ready?"

"In about an hour."

"Will it be ruined if we put it off another half hour?"

"What for?"

"We're getting another mouth to feed."

She sighed. "Whose now?"

"Jeff's."

The sigh turned into a smile. "It can wait."

"Don't tell the kids. Let's surprise them."

Complaints of hunger increased by the minute. There were saucers of nuts and Christmas candy all over the place, but nobody would touch them and risk denting his appetite. Marilyn kept thinking of different reasons for the delay. Finally I saw a car pull up. Another boy was driving; Jeff was in the front seat with him, a girl was in the backseat. Jeff got out quickly and started running up the driveway to the back of the house.

I called out, "Okay, kids, dinner is ready. Everybody into the dining room! Come on, let's go. Hurry up now!" The kids couldn't understand the sudden rush act after all the stalling, but I managed to get them all into the dining room and at their places while Marilyn held Jeff in the kitchen.

When I went out there he began, "Listen, Dad, I'm sorry. I shouldn't have—"

"We'll talk it over later," I said. "Give me your coat." As he removed his coat, I pointed to the turkey cooling on the table.

"That turkey weighs twenty-two pounds. Can you carry it?"

"Sure."

"Then you take it into the dining room and put it in front of my place."

Marilyn wasn't sure. "Bill, suppose they rush him and he drops it?"

"Then we'll eat off the floor. Go ahead, son." I could see

that he liked the idea. He picked up the tray and headed for the door.

All the kids went crazy—even Barbara.

It was a good Christmas. It is always good when people discover that they love each other.

# 11

Barbara's parents were so eager to see her that they left their home on Christmas night and drove straight through, reaching our home December 26, just as my family was beginning to stir. We had a second Christmas as we watched Barbara open the presents they had brought. I kept wishing that she would show more reaction to seeing her parents, more pleasure, more delight with the gifts.

Around ten, I invited her father to inspect our office layout. Over coffee in my office, I gave him the background of the foundation, emphasizing the spiritual aspects, and was gingerly approaching the whole topic of demons and demon possession, not knowing how much exposure he'd had to this subject, when the telephone rang. Judy had recently started working as my secretary; now she stuck her head around the door and said, "Dad, it's Leonard Evans." I assumed that Leonard was merely checking to see if Barbara's parents had arrived safely; however, I quickly heard the sadness in his voice. Barbara's paternal grandfather had died during the night; would I convey the news to her father?

I said, "Leonard, Barbara's father is right here in my office with me." As I handed him the phone, I said, "Leonard has some bad news for you." Then I left the room and shut the door.

He remained in my office about ten minutes; when he came out he was red-eyed but composed. I offered my sympathy.

He nodded. "Thanks. We'll have to head right back, of course."

"Yes."

"Can we take Barbara?"

"Of course. I just hope you can get her to come back to us. We think a lot of her around here."

"She'll come back. I promise it. Right after the funeral."

We went into the house. It was a shock to everyone, of course, even to us who had not known the man; the only person who didn't show any real emotion was, again, Barbara.

After the three of them left, I asked Jeff to come down to my office, and we had a talk. He told me that he hadn't gone to his parents' home on Christmas Eve. He had gone to the home of the boy who had picked him up, the same boy who brought him back the next day; the girl in the backseat was the boy's sister. I asked, "Can you tell me why you did it, Jeff?"

"I don't know, Dad," he said. "When I asked if I could go home and you said no, I wasn't too disappointed. I knew Christmas would be great here. But then you told me how Shirley's parents and Barbara's parents had called you and wanted their kids home. I got to thinking about that. My parents hadn't called about me going home for Christmas. I guess I just got mad."

Bill Bair, I said to myself, you're a blabbermouthed fool who talks too much. "Jeff," I said aloud, "your folks were just following the rules. Of course they wanted you home, but they knew what the agreement was. Look at all the presents they sent you!"

"Sure," he shrugged, "they're always giving me stuff."

"There's something else I want to talk to you about," I hurried on. "After Ted goes back to Pittsburgh next week, things will be pretty quiet around here for you, won't they?"

"Ted will be home on weekends," he said.

"Most weekends. Even so, there's all week to think about."

"Herbert will be here. He's okay."

"I think I've got a love home for Herbert, near Pittsburgh. People who've been after me for a boy for a long time," I said. "And, Jeff, for that matter, I think I've got a place for you."

"Someplace else for me to live?"

"Yes."

"Are you putting me out, Dad? Are you punishing me?"

I shook my head. "In the first place, Jeff, you know how the foundation works. You knew when you came here that you were going to stay only long enough to get your bearings. In the second place, if I wanted to punish you, I certainly wouldn't suggest that you move in with one of the finest families we have."

"Who?"

"The Cobbs. They've got a terrific farm about twenty miles out of town. And they've got two sons around your age. The foundation has already placed a couple of boys with the Cobbs, and the kids had a great time. As far as Ted is concerned, you'll probably see as much of him at the Cobbs' as you would here. There's great hunting out there, so he goes there a lot. I'll tell you what. Before I say a word to the Cobbs, I'll have Ted take you out there for a day, and then you can tell me whether you'd like to live with them. Okay?"

"I went against your way once, Dad," he said, "and I was miserable. I won't go against you again."

"Jeff," I said, "I wish everybody could learn as quick as you, and be as gracious about it."

I was sure Jeff was ready for the move to another home, but about Herbert I didn't feel so certain. In spite of his sincere commitment to Christ, he was still a pretty defenseless and insecure little fellow. The background of fear and abuse was going to take time to get over: whenever the smallest thing went wrong the enormous round tears still started flowing.

The trouble was, after the holiday lull, eight new kids were due here next week, more the week after that, and we were going to need every bed we had. When Marilyn and the other foundation directors and I had prayed about a home for Herbert, the name that kept coming up was the Petersons, who had a farm near Pittsburgh. I called them now, and when I told them about Herbert they were ready to come and pick him up right away. I said I'd prefer to have him stay with us through the holidays; I'd drive him down myself the weekend before school reopened. I decided not to say anything to Herbert for a few days. Those big tears took too much out of me. But I did think it would be a good idea to start talking up farm life to him.

Shirley's was still a different situation. Since Christmas Eve she'd been literally a transformed person—radiating her newfound happiness. And, unlike Herbert, Shirley had a stable home to return to. I almost wondered if she was going to need the transition period in a foster home. I decided to make no decision about Shirley yet, not until I saw how she behaved with her parents, not until I saw continuing evidence of the strength of her commitment.

As for Barbara, the decision seemed to have been taken out of our hands: the Hamners had called twice in the past two days asking when they could have her. Because I felt they had a right to know everything we did, I drove out to see them one afternoon. I gave them Barbara's history—the witchcraft, the hypnosis, the sex, the hospitalizations, the suicide attempts, the possibility that she was possessed by demons. The Hamners were heart-stricken about the possibility of possession. I told the Hamners about Don Basham, whom they had heard preach when he had a pastorate in this area. I said that he was on his way for a visit and that when Barbara came back—if she came back—we would ask him to try deliverance. At the end of our discussion they were as eager to add Barbara to their family as ever before.

I got home to find two enormous hams sitting in a cardboard box in the driveway. There was an envelope with them addressed to the Bairs, but the Christmas card inside was unsigned. That sort of thing kept happening all week. One morning we found two big capons in a shopping bag on the back porch. Then a woman called and said she had four gallons of turkey stew and four gallons of chili we could have if we wanted. We wanted. As it turned out, despite all the company, I only had to shell out seventeen extra dollars to fill in the gaps in the menus. We did a lot of praising the Lord that week.

Three days after Christmas, Shirley's parents arrived. What a difference from their first visit when they'd had to prod her up the walk. Shirley was still so high on her commitment to the Lord that she told them about it when they were scarcely out of the car. They kept staring at her as though wondering if this was the same girl they'd left with us only three weeks before. When the time came to start preparing supper, Shirley's mother pitched right in like an old neighbor.

Around five, Don Basham called. "Bill, we're still over a hundred miles from New Wilmington. Go ahead and eat; we'll stop somewhere along the road."

I said, "Don't you dare. Marilyn is laying out a spread big enough for a John Wesley revival."

I reported to Marilyn. "That was Don Basham on the phone. They want to stop for supper on the road."

Exasperation exploded on her face. "Oh, Bill—all this food. Oh, I feel like having a fit."

I kissed her. "That's what I told Don, so they changed their minds and they're coming in."

She frowned at me. "You know, Papa Bair, there are times when you give me fits, too."

We let the kids eat early. It was after seven when the Bashams arrived and then the kids had seconds while the grown-ups and the five Basham young folks made our first assault on the massive buffet. And still there were leftovers.

The next morning I talked to Don about Barbara. As I

went over the details, Don would nod once in a while, recognizing certain clues, certain symptoms. "It sure sounds possible to me," he admitted. "When are you expecting Barbara back?"

"Two or three days at the latest. I just hope it wasn't a mistake, letting her go away right now."

Later that morning, Geert Steenwyk called from New York where he had just landed from Holland: he had a reservation on a flight that would get him into Pittsburgh in the late afternoon. Could anybody pick him up? I said I would and telephoned the Petersons to see if I could stop by with Herbert on the way so they could meet him. I had to make them promise that they wouldn't say a word about his moving in with them; I still hadn't brought myself to broach the subject to him.

At the lunch table I turned to Herbert. "Son, I have to go to Pittsburgh this afternoon. Would you like to come along and keep me company?"

"I sure would," he said. I always tried to take one of the kids along, just by himself, when I had a drive to make: every child needs to be singled out this way from time to time, relieved of the sense of being part of a mob. In this case, however, I had an ulterior motive as well and I felt a pang of guilt as I saw Herbert's eagerness.

I didn't mention the Petersons until we were about ten miles from their place. Then I asked, "Herbert, do you like horses?"

"I sure do," he said.

"Have you ever ridden one?"

"No."

"Would you like to?"

"I sure would."

"Well, Herbert," I said, "I have some friends who live just up ahead. They have a beautiful farm. Let's stop off and visit them and maybe they'll let you ride one of their horses."

The Petersons had two daughters, grown now, married and living away. They very much wanted a child in the house, and they particularly wanted a boy. It had seemed to all of us who knew Herbert that he was one of those exceptions to our rule of placing young people in homes where there were kids their own age: here was a love-starved youngster who could use the undivided attention he would receive as an only child.

It is always a touching experience for me to watch prospective foster parents meet a prospective foster child for the first time, and the Petersons followed the pattern. They couldn't take their eyes off Herbert. They couldn't stop touching him, couldn't stop smiling at him. Although he and I had left the dining table not more than an hour before, the Petersons had a big meal ready for us, and Herbert went at the food as though he hadn't eaten for a week. They kept piling up his plate. I mentioned that Herbert was eager to ride a horse. Jeff Peterson was at the door in two steps, shouting something about saddling up Old Paint in the barn. I hurried to his side where I could speak in a whisper. "Find a gentle one for him, Jeff," I pleaded. "He's never even been on one before."

When Herbert finally couldn't eat any more, he and Jeff went outside. Emma Peterson and I watched through the front-room window as Jeff helped Herbert mount a horse that looked like a senile veteran from a milk company.

Emma said, "Bill, we've got to have that boy. He's ador-able."

I replied, "He also sheds the biggest tears you've ever seen. They can break your heart. Be ready for a lot of them when I bring him here next week."

When Herbert and I were back in the car, heading for the airport, I asked, "Did you have a good time at the Petersons'?"

"I sure did," he said.

"Would you like to go back there again?"

"I sure would. Let's go back there again someday, Dad."

I said, "The Petersons are lonely, Herbert, with their own children grown up. While you were out riding, Mrs. Peterson told me how much they'd like to have a young person in the house again. Any boy living on a ranch like that would be very lucky, wouldn't he?"

He shot me a quick glance. "I guess so."

"You know he would."

He said, "Maybe you can find somebody for them." He looked straight ahead and didn't say much after that.

The excitement of the airport brought Herbert out of his mood. We went up on the promenade and watched the planes arriving and departing. When Geert's flight was called, we went to his gate and waited for him. Herbert sat between us on the drive home while Geert regaled us with an account of Christmas in Holland. As we passed the turnoff to the Petersons' I said, "Hey, Geert, on the way to the airport, Herbert and I stopped off to visit the Petersons. And guess what? Herbert got his first ride on a horse."

Geert said, "That's terrific. Did you enjoy it, Herbert?"

Herbert said, "Yeah."

I said, "Herbert had a wonderful time. He wants to go back and visit the Petersons again. Don't you, Herbert?"

Herbert said, "Yeah."

Over Herbert's head, Geert's eyes asked me a question, and I nodded. Geert said, "I don't blame you, Herbert. The Petersons are wonderful people. I visit them a lot myself. Did you like them, Herbert?"

Herbert said, "Sorta."

It wasn't until the next morning in the office that I had the chance to fill Geert in on Herbert's background. Geert agreed that as long as Herbert's father continued to drink so heavily we could not send the boy home. "I'll start making some visits to the family," Geert said, "and find out how badly they want to straighten things out. Anyway, I think you've made a good choice with the Petersons. They'll love him until he's spoiled rotten."

That morning Ted and Jeff had headed out early to the Cobbs' for a day of hunting; I drove over after supper to pick them up. The minute I saw Jeff in the Cobb kitchen I knew there'd be no trouble about this move. He'd made himself completely at home, at the moment was drying dishes with the two Cobb boys. When the time came to leave, Bud Cobb went out to the freezer and came back with a cardboard box. "I did some butchering last week," he said. "There're twenty-six steaks here, Bill."

I said, "Thank you, Bud. The Lord will bless you for this."

"I think He already has," Bud said, and I caught his glance at Jeff.

Jeff shook hands with the two Cobb boys and said he'd see them around. He shook hands with Bud Cobb and thanked him for the great hunting. But when he got to Nora Cobb, he leaned over suddenly and kissed her on the cheek. "Thanks very much, Mrs. Cobb, for letting me come out. I had a wonderful time."

Nora was beaming. "Come back anytime, Jeff. The place is yours."

Heading back to town, I said, "It looked to me like you had a good time with the Cobbs, Jeff."

"The best time of my life," he said. "The Cobbs are great people. They're the greatest people I ever met, next to the Bairs."

I said, "The Bairs won't mind taking second place to the Cobbs. Have you given any thought to my idea?"

"About moving in with them?"

"Yes."

Jeff said, "I don't think that's the question."

"What's the question, then?"

"The question is, do the Cobbs want me to move in?"

I said, "You know I promised I wouldn't say anything to them until you'd looked them over. But it seemed to me that they liked you fine."

"The Cobbs are the kind of people who like everybody," said Jeff. "But when you want to have some kid move in with you, you've got to like him special."

Ted said, "I think the Cobbs like you special, Jeff. I've been there hundreds of times, and I never got the kind of treatment you got from the minute you set foot in the place."

"That was because it was my first time," Jeff said. He was obviously getting himself ready for a letdown.

Ted said, "I think you're wrong. In fact, I'll bet on it. I'll bet, Jeff, that the Cobbs will call Dad right away—

tonight—about you. If I lose, you get my steak for supper tomorrow night. If I win, I get yours."

"It's a bet," Jeff said. "You're the witness, Dad."

As we opened the front door, Marilyn called out, "Did you forget something at the Cobbs'? Nora just called. She wants you to call her back right away."

I looked at the boys. Jeff put the box of steaks on the kitchen table, not meeting my eyes. I picked up the wall phone and dialed the Cobbs' number. Nora answered on the first ring. "What's up, Nora?" I asked.

She said, "Bill, we just wanted to tell you again how much we enjoyed having Ted and Jeff with us for the day."

"They enjoyed it, too," I said.

"We were wondering—are you going to place Jeff in a love home?"

"Sooner or later."

"Have you got one in mind?"

"Sort of."

"Well, Bill, I was going to call you about this tomorrow, but the boys insisted that I call tonight. We sure would love to have Jeff come and live with us."

"Can't blame you for that, Nora."

"What are our chances, Bill?"

"I'd say they're pretty good."

"Have you any idea how Jeff might feel about it?"

"Why don't you ask him?" I handed the phone to Jeff and heard his side of the conversation.

" 'Lo? Mrs. Cobb? I had a wonderful time, too, best time of my life. Yes, I guess I'll be moving someday. You do? Do you all feel that way? Well, gee, Mom, yes. Yes. I really mean it. But, Mom, can I stay here until Ted goes back to school?

He's my best friend. Next Saturday, I think. Yes. Thanks, Mom. Yes. Okay, Mom. Good night. And say good night to Dad for me, will you, and the guys?"

He hung up. He couldn't look at us. I wondered how long it was going to take for the tears to come. I knew I was pretty close myself. It's a sight to behold, when a lonely kid finds out that people are crazy about him.

Ted said, "Jeff, you just lost yourself a steak."

Jeff swallowed. He said, "I don't care. Where I'm going, I can get all the steak I want."

"What's all this about steaks?" Marilyn asked.

Ted pointed to the box. "The Cobbs gave us half a cow."

I added, "And they got themselves a son."

Jeff was getting very close now. As Ted and I slipped out of the room, I got a glimpse of Marilyn stepping to him and taking him into her arms.

The next morning, while I was going over the mail, Shirley and her parents came to my office. "Bill," Shirley's mother began, "we've decided to start for home after lunch."

"I'm sorry to hear that," I said. "Can't you stay longer?"

"We'd like to, Bill," said Shirley's dad, "but I've got to get back to my job."

"I can understand that," I said, "but you're going to miss out on a great steak dinner."

Shirley's mother leaned forward a bit. "Bill, we would like to take Shirley home with us today. Is it possible?"

I looked at Shirley. "How do you feel about it, honey?"

"I'd like to go," she said. "I'm very grateful to you for everything you've done for me. You've changed my life. You've saved my life."

"The Lord did that. We just stood around and watched."

"I know, but if I hadn't come here—"

"The Lord did that, too."

"I know. Anyway, I would like to go home, but I'll stay if you think I should."

I prayed for the right words. I asked Shirley, "Don't your home schools have a new term that begins around the first of February?"

"Yes."

"Do you plan on going back to school?"

"Yes."

"Those friends of yours with the motorcycles—do they go to the same school?"

"Most of them don't go to school. I met them at a place downtown where kids hang out."

"I hope you never go back there."

She shook her head. "I don't need that place anymore."

"I'll tell you what I'd like you to do, Shirley," I said. "Jeff and Herbert will be moving out on us in a few days. And when Barbara gets back there's a family that's been pestering us to let her go to their place. But a whole batch of new kids is coming next week. I'd appreciate it if you would stay with us to help them get settled—just until you have to go home for the new semester. Will you do that as a favor to me?"

I could see she was disappointed, but she tried to smile as she said, "Of course, Papa Bair. If you think I can do some good around here, I'll be happy to stay."

"Thank you," I said. "I appreciate that." Another month would do a lot to confirm her in her brand-new life.

Barbara returned from New Jersey that afternoon. Since he had known her in the days when they both attended

Leonard Evans's church, Geert went to the airport to meet her. He was shocked at the total personality change; he said she'd sat with her head bowed most of the drive home, scarcely responding to his questions. At the house she would not come down for supper, saying she'd eaten on the plane. I was heartsick, fearing that the funeral—the whole visit home with its errand of death—had pushed her deeper into her unhealthy fantasies.

The Bashams were out that day visiting old friends in the area, and by the time they got back to our place, Barbara was in bed.

"Did you ever feel you'd gotten through to her, Bill?" Don asked when we'd described her current frame of mind. "Before she went home, I mean."

I said, "The only time she showed any normal human feelings was when she broke down in my arms that time. After that she seemed to come out of her shell a little—she'd come down and watch television and she'd come to the table for meals. But she never really joined the family."

Don sighed. "Well, maybe I can talk to her in the morning."

But as it turned out we didn't have to wait that long. At four in the morning, Jeanne woke us up to say that Barbara was once again locked in the bathroom and was threatening to kill herself. I got Don up and together we stood outside the locked door.

"Come on out, Barbara," I said. "Open the door and come out. We've got someone here who can help you. Please come out."

From inside: "I'm going to kill myself."

I said, "You know you won't do that. You told me yourself you can't."

She said, "I can do it this time. This time, I'm going to."

Don touched me on the shoulder and I moved aside. He leaned close to the door; his voice was conversational, warm. He said, "Barbara, my name is Don Basham. I want to help you. Barbara, I think I know what is troubling you. You keep doing things you don't want to do, don't you? You keep being driven to do things that you know are wrong, but you can't stop yourself. You think the only way you can stop doing these things is to kill yourself. That's what the voices are saying to you, isn't it? You're not alone in the bathroom, are you? The others are there with you. You have some idea who they are, but you've been too afraid to admit it, even to yourself. How long have they tormented you, Barbara? Did it begin that night when you were hypnotized? Barbara, the voices want you to die. But Jesus wants you to live. Jesus wants to set you free, Barbara. Come out, now. Let Him help you."

We waited. Perhaps a minute passed. Then we heard the door being unlocked. Barbara stepped out, her face invisible behind a wild tangle of hair. "How do you know these things?" she whispered.

"The Holy Spirit shows them to me. And He shows me something else. He shows me that Jesus is more powerful than all the evil, hateful voices in the world. Jesus can send these things out of your life forever, Barbara."

The trembling I had noticed so often had started again at the name "Jesus." But this time Barbara herself seemed to be making an effort against it. "Is that true?" she asked in a low, strangled voice.

"It's true, Barbara. Only you must want Him to do it."

"I do! I do!" She was sobbing now, trembling harder than ever.

During the Bashams' visit, four girls were sharing the room across the hall; now the other three tactfully evacuated it as we led Barbara in and shut the door behind us. First Don said a short prayer asking God's help and protection in what we were about to do. Then he led Barbara in a confession of her involvement with horoscopes and other occult practices in New Jersey. "When you did those things, Barbara, you were opening the door and inviting these ugly things into your life. Now they'll stick by their rights. They've come by invitation and not even the power of God can make them leave while you hold that door open. Confession is just the start. Repeat after me, 'I *renounce* witchcraft. I *renounce* Ouija boards. I *renounce* hypnotism. . . .' "

It was a long list, but Barbara's voice grew stronger as she continued. "I renounce anger . . . hate . . . deceit . . . vengeance. . . ."

When it was all over a new voice spoke out, a voice I had never heard before—the clear, lilting, laughing voice of a young girl caught by surprise.

"They're gone. They're all gone! I'm just me."

I opened my eyes. It was Barbara speaking, but not in the lifeless monotone which was all I had heard from her until this moment. She stood up, brushing her hair from her face, and smiled at us. She was the most beautiful girl I'd ever seen.

"Praise Jesus, Barbara," Don was saying. "Thank Him for what He has done for you."

As naturally as a child bubbling over to her father, Barbara lifted up her head and began to pray. Neither Don nor I could understand a word. The Spirit had filled Barbara, and she was praising the Lord in tongues.

If I'd ever had any doubts about the reality of demon oppression and the effectiveness of the deliverance ministry, the next few days with Barbara dispelled them all. She was another person, the person Geert said he recalled from his previous knowledge of her, but with an extra sparkle that was the Spirit's own. She couldn't do enough around the house as we all packed away Christmas ornaments and swept up tinsel and pine needles—listening to her laugh was like having Christmas all over again. I began to wonder if she, too, might not be ready for an early return home, but Don advised against it. "These occult groups are jealous as all get-out once someone 'belongs to them,' as they see it. I don't know anything about the people she was seeing in New Jersey—except I'm sure she hasn't heard the last of them. She'd better be grounded pretty solidly in her new life before she goes back."

So it was agreed that Barbara would go to the Hamners at least for a few months. And meanwhile the very day had come for Herbert to go to the Petersons', and still neither Marilyn nor I had been able to speak to him about moving out.

"*I* can't do it," said Marilyn. "He'll start walking around with those big tears streaming down his face, and I'll change my mind in a minute."

I said, "You know, I'd be happy to keep Herbert with us."

"So would I," she said, "but we always feel that way about

every child that comes here. If we start giving in we may as well forget the foundation."

"You're right," I admitted, "but I'm sure not looking forward to this."

Jeff, too, was leaving us that day. He was no problem. He'd been phoning the Cobbs every day, and the Cobb boys had been by to visit him twice. Geert had offered to drive Jeff out to the farm, but the Cobbs insisted on picking him up themselves, and they were at the house before the milkman got there. Jeff's departure was all jokes and laughter, and his last words were to Ted: "You're going to come and visit me, remember?"

Ted said, "Right. And you're going to come and visit me." They said good-bye on that.

When the car was out of sight I said to Ted, "Son, I'll drive you back to school whenever you're ready."

"Thanks, Dad," he said.

"What time do you want to leave?"

"I'd like to be there for lunch."

"Around ten o'clock, then." I looked at Herbert. "Herbert, would you like to come along for the ride?"

"I sure would," he said.

I hated doing this. I said, "Listen, Herbert, we'll be passing the Peterson farm. Would you like to stop off there and ride a horse again?"

"I sure would."

I braced myself. "Herbert, the Petersons have been after me to let you stay with them for a few days. Why don't you take along some clothes so that you can do that."

"Clothes?"

"Yes. If you're going to stay with them, you'll want your things with you, won't you?"

"Stay with them?" Two big tears started out of his eyes.

I had to look away. "Yes. You can stay with them just as long as you're enjoying yourself. If you don't like it after you've tried it, you can phone me and I'll come and get you."

After a moment I glanced at him. His shirt was polka dotted with tears. He went slowly up the stairs to the third floor.

When an hour passed and Herbert still hadn't come back down, I sent Joni to get him. She was back in a minute. "He's not up there."

Ted came into the living room with his suitcase. "Did you try under the bed?" he asked. "Never mind, Joni, let me handle this." We gave Ted half an hour to minister to Herbert; then I called up and said we'd better be on our way. The tears flowed again as Marilyn helped Herbert into his coat and kissed him good-bye. Then he went around the room, saying good-bye to the girls, sending each one of them in turn running from the room, sobbing. That's the awful thing about being able to love so much—you hurt too easily.

The Petersons were expecting us and had a big dinner ready. I told them I had to get Ted into Pittsburgh by noon and we couldn't stay. I wanted to get out of there.

Emma Peterson asked, "Bill, what do we do about those tears?"

I said, "Get him on a horse right away. And if he disappears, look for him under beds."

About an hour later, heading back, I passed the Petersons' road and thought of stopping in. Then I decided against it, feeling it would be better for Herbert to get used to being without the Bairs as soon as possible. And about an hour after that, when I was perhaps fifteen miles from New Wilmington, I recognized Geert's car coming toward me. As he passed, he blared his horn and signaled me to stop. In my rearview mirror, I saw Geert make a u-turn. I pulled over.

When Geert got to me, he said, "The Petersons just called. Herbert ran away about half an hour ago."

"Are they sure?" I asked, heart-struck. "Did they check under the beds?"

"Yes," Geert said. "He's gone. He took his suitcase."

"You better head back to our place," I said. "The new kids could be arriving any time before supper. I'll get started on this."

I turned around and raced back down the highway. My main concern was that Herbert might have headed into Pittsburgh, looking for Ted.

But about three miles short of the Peterson turnoff, walking in the direction of New Wilmington, I saw him on the far side of the road. I pulled up and got out, waited until the traffic eased; then crossed the road and quickstepped the distance to Herbert, who was still trudging along. I said, "Herbert, let me have your suitcase." I don't think he'd seen me, yet he didn't seem especially surprised to have me show up. I've learned that most kids who run away in these circumstances are hoping that they'll be found before they get too far. When the traffic allowed, we crossed and got into my car.

The tears were beginning again. I asked, "Herbert, why did you run away from the Petersons?"

"I don't want to stay there."

"That's a good reason but it's not a fair one," I said. "You haven't given them a chance. You had a good time when you were there the last time, didn't you?"

"That was a visit. It wasn't staying there."

"Have I said that you had to stay there?"

"No."

"Well, you don't. And that's a promise. But I do want you to visit them for a few days. If you like them and they like you, you can stay. If you don't like each other, they'll be just as happy as you to say good-bye. But I want you to give them a chance. Will you do that for me?"

"I want to stay with you."

I said, "Herbert, do you remember, on Christmas Eve, when you committed your life to Jesus?"

"Yes."

"That was a beautiful thing to do and you made us all very happy. Do you know why we were happy?"

No answer.

"Because, Herbert, when you did that, it meant that from then on Jesus was the most important person in your life. Not me, or Mama Bair, or even your own family. It meant that wherever you were, whoever you were with, the Person you love most, and who loves you most, could always be right beside you, helping you, making you strong. Isn't that right?"

"I guess so."

"Well, how do you think Jesus feels now, when the first time you have a little difficulty you come running to the Bairs instead of to Him?"

"I dunno."

"He feels hurt, I can tell you that."

"This morning," said Herbert, "Ted said he was going to go and visit Jeff at the Cobbs'."

"Well?"

"Ted didn't say that he would come and visit me at the Petersons'."

"Do you want him to?"

"Yes."

"Then why didn't you say so? Ted is no mind reader, you know."

"Would he visit me?"

"I'll tell you what, Herbert," I said. "Let's go back to the Petersons' house. First, I want you to apologize to them for running away and making them worry. Then we'll call Ted at his school and see when he can come and visit you."

I didn't know how the Lord felt about Herbert's friendship priorities, but I was sure that He was listening to our conversation, so I did what I felt Jesus would have done at that moment. I put my arms around Herbert and hugged him.

All this was nearly three years ago—the very day that Jimmy, Carl, Pete, and Susie entered our house and our lives. A few days later, Richard and Debbie joined us, then Phyllis and Sally. So many wonderful kids, so many wonderful times—but that would take another book.

Shirley stayed with us until the end of January, when she returned home to enter high school. She seemed to enjoy the month working with the newcomers, especially the younger ones. She also took off another five pounds in the Bair Jogging and Fruit for Dessert Club. The day I drove her to the airport, she said in the car, "Papa Bair, I think I know what I want to do with my life. I want to work with children."

"There's no work that could make you happier."

"I've been thinking about it. I think that when I finish college, if you'd let me, I'd like to come back here and work for the foundation."

"If we'd let you!" I said. "Honey, I can't think of a greater break for us!"

Shirley's in her second year of college now, and we're keeping in touch so that if she still wants to do this when she's finished, her courses will meet all the state requirements.

Jeff stayed with the Cobbs until September. Geert and I had several visits with his parents. Jeff's father found it was impossible to avoid evening appointments in his business, but he worked it out to keep most weekends free to spend with his son. Jeff's mother was for chucking her interior decorating business altogether, but since it was obvious that she was good at it and in great demand, Geert and I were able to convince her that the Lord wants us to use the talents He gives us. In June, she was able to hire a young woman who had just graduated from an interior design school in New York to cover appointments in late afternoons and evenings, allowing Jeff's mother to be home when he is. Jeff continues to be part of the Cobb family too; the kids are always visiting back and forth, and Jeff spends part of his summer vacations at the farm. The Cobbs have another foundation boy with them now, and Jeff keeps telling him how lucky he is.

We were unable to be of any help to Herbert's father. Like so many alcoholics, the man denied that he had a drinking problem, would not attend AA meetings, or see a doctor. When we found out that he did not have a permit for the revolver he had in the house, we were able to get the police to take it away from him. Herbert is still with the Petersons. When he finishes high school, he wants to go into farming full time.

Barbara turned out to be not much of a letter writer after she got back to New Jersey in June, although the Hamner girls still hear occasionally. Most of our news came through Leonard Evans, glowing reports of her continuing health and growth. About a year ago, Marilyn and I paid a surprise visit to the Bible college Barbara's attending now. We came upon her unexpectedly in a hallway. When she saw us she dropped her books and papers all over the floor, and we hugged and cried and just let the other students stare.

And the Bairs are going strong. Ted is married, and is serving in the navy. He and his wife have made us grand-parents. Marty recently married a boy she knew in high school; he's teaching school himself now in Ohio. They want to start a love home; but we tell them to give the twosome a chance for a while. Judy is working as a dental assistant in New Castle and is still a very important part of the Bair home. Joni and Jeanne are almost ready for college.

As for Marilyn and me, life just seems to get fuller, richer, and more exciting every year. The original vision of provid-ing a place for kids who didn't have one has become a bigger dream. It's a dream of America emptying its institu-tions for children by opening its homes. It's a vision of love homes, Christian homes open to children in every city and town and village in the land.

Wherever I go around the country to speak about the

foundation, people ask me, "Could we do it here?" and I say, "Why not?" It doesn't take vast sums of money. It doesn't take a big organization. It doesn't take any more professional supervision than most communities have available. It does take a group of Christians who are willing to support one another in prayer. It takes a lot of love. It takes a lot of leaning on the Lord.

But there's a funny thing about that. The more you lean on Him, the straighter He seems to make you stand. The more you let His love act through you, the more He showers on you to give away.

# 12

More than four years have come and gone since the last chapter was written. I'm sitting on the patio of our home, overlooking the lake, and I find myself reflecting on the many miracles that have happened since then. I can't help but remember, too, some of the major obstacles that have threatened the survival of our work, including a serious breakdown in communication that nearly destroyed Marilyn's and my marriage.

Good news first. The house is quieter now, but the Bair Foundation is busier than ever, and our new administration building next door is bustling with more activity than Marilyn and I ever thought possible 11 years ago when God first spoke to me at Neshannock Presbyterian Church.

So much has happened that I hardly know where to begin. Maybe the best place is a few months after that busy Christmastime when we had so many guests. Shirley returned home, and for a while Marilyn and I were alone with our four girls—Marty, Judy, Jeanne and Joni. Ted had joined the Navy. Then the Lord brought Gayle into our lives.

Gayle was given up by her natural family when she was five, and had been a ward of the county ever since. Because she had never known much love, she felt very little self-worth, and had never learned to love anyone else. So Gayle had withdrawn emotionally, and expressed her hurt outwardly through rebellion.

It was rebellion that caused a succession of foster homes to give her up, sometimes after only a few days. Now, at 16, Gayle had been in and out of 18 foster homes.

I'll never forget the day the caseworker from the county brought her over. It was a beautiful afternoon in July, and Geert and I were sitting on the front porch of our house on Nesshannock Avenue as the car drove up. Out stepped one of the most beautiful girls I have ever seen. Her blond hair shone in the sun—but her skirt was so short it scarcely covered her thighs. She met our greetings with a direct, unwavering stare.

After Geert and I explained what the love homes were all about, I told her she would be living with the Bairs for a while. And I added that her outfit was not suitable attire, and that we expected her to dress more modestly.

Gayle nodded, but as she stared at me, I wondered if a challenge was in the offing.

It came the following morning. Gayle didn't come downstairs until the rest of us were already seated at the breakfast table, waiting to say grace. Conversation was lively, and the girls were planning the day's activities.

Then Gayle came through the kitchen, dressed in a pair of black satin jumper shorts that were so tight they showed every crease in her body. Her walk was rebellious, and her eyes were fixed on me. All conversation at the table ceased, and four more pairs of eyes turned to me with the unspoken question: What will Daddy do?

I said in a casual voice, "Gayle, I want you to go back

upstairs and change into something more appropriate.''

Her response was quick, her tone full of hostility: ''You're not telling me what to do.'' And she stared at me, hands on her hips.

I shot up a quick prayer for wisdom. Then I stood up.

''I think we should both go into the living room for a talk,'' I said, managing to keep my voice even. ''Go ahead and say grace, the rest of you.''

She followed me reluctantly into the next room.

''Gayle,'' I began as we sat down on the sofa, ''do you remember our conversation yesterday afternoon out on the porch?''

Gayle's eyes glittered. ''I remember.''

''Well, I want to remind you that whatever situations you've had in the past, you're part of our family now. We don't even consider you a foster daughter, but one of our own children. But I don't allow any of my daughters to dress the way you're dressed, and I'm not going to permit it from you either. Now go upstairs and put on something more presentable.''

Gayle finally lowered her eyes. ''I don't have anything different,'' she said in a sulky voice.

''All right,'' I said, ''then for now you'll simply have to let the hem out of the shorts you're wearing.''

Gayle took a minute to consider this, then rose without a word and left the room. Her expression left no doubt as to the contempt she felt—for me and for her new life as a member of the Bair family. I rejoined the others at the breakfast table wondering what was to be the outcome of this battle of wills.

Every day after that brought a conflict in one thing or another. Clothes were a continual problem. No sooner had Gayle let the hem out of one outfit than she would shorten something else. When Marilyn asked her to do some job around the house, Gayle would agree to it—and never get around to doing it.

After so many years of rejection, Gayle was afraid to let anyone get close to her. We showed her love in as many ways as we could, but she didn't know how to receive it, and she wouldn't allow herself to express any love in return. I knew that, deep inside Gayle longed to be part of a loving family. But for months she remained outwardly withdrawn, saying little and spending long hours alone in her room.

Then we began to notice chinks in her armor. She began opening up to the girls. And a couple of incidents in particular let me know that Gayle was at last beginning to respond.

Once I overheard Gayle call Marilyn "Mom" as they were doing dishes together. Another time when I telephoned home, Gayle answered with a tentative "Hi, Dad." I knew then that we were winning her trust.

It began to be clear why Gayle had a hard time accepting our love. One evening she looked troubled, and I asked her if something was on her mind.

Gayle hesitated. Finally she said, "You know, I like it here with you and Mama Bair and my four sisters. But does that mean that I don't love my own parents anymore?" She hadn't lived with her natural parents in more than ten years, yet she had been troubled by the fear that she was betraying them!

"Oh, honey, it doesn't mean that at all," I assured her, and I went on to explain how Gayle could learn to be a more loving daughter to her own parents by giving and receiving love in the Bair family right now.

That was a turning point in Gayle's life with us. I walked away from our conversation that day knowing she was in the midst of a change. I already had a special relationship with her, and I knew she was eager to gain my approval. But I felt it wouldn't be long before that desire was put to the test.

Several weeks later Gayle brought Don home for the first time. Gayle had been living with us for about two years by then, and was working as a secretary for a large insurance firm. One afternoon as I was working in my office, I heard a car in the driveway. I glanced out the window.

There, getting out of a recent-model sedan, was Gayle, accompanied by a bearded youth with long hair, faded blue jeans, black motorcycle jacket and heavy boots. My heart sank—and before I knew it I had fallen into the old trap of judging someone by their outward appearance instead of seeing the person inside.

*This rebellious-looking young man can't be any good for our Dee,* I thought to myself, *and I'm going to let her know it.*

I heard her ask him to wait outside; then she came breezing through the front door. I knew she was looking for me. But as I met her outside the door to my office, all my disappointment and anger rose to the surface.

"Where did you pick him up?" I asked.

"Oh, Dad, he's really nice!" she bubbled. "His name is Don. I met him downtown after work."

"I suppose he's part of a motorcycle gang?"

"Of course he's not," she said, her smile dimming. "He works at the supermarket. Don't you want to come out and meet him?"

"Gayle, you know I don't like you hanging around with boys like him."

A look of pain crossed Gayle's face. Then her eyes brimmed with tears, and she turned and flew up the stairs two at a time. I heard the bedroom door slam behind her.

I realized it was up to me to make conversation with Don until Gayle came down. So I wandered outside, feeling out-of-sorts. Don was leaning against his car, and he looked up as I approached.

"Where do you go to church?" I asked.

"I'm Catholic," he replied.

How often do you attend Mass?"

"That's my business." And he began scraping a spot on the hood of the car with his fingernail.

We stood in silence for a few minutes after that, until Gayle came out. She looked herself again, even though her eyes were a little red. But I noticed that her desire for my approval was being overcome by an even stronger assurance that this boy was someone special.

Don came around regularly after that. He was a quiet, thoughtful young man, and I soon learned that his tough appearance was just a cover-up for insecurity. He was looking for love and approval, just as Gayle had been.

One night in November, Don arrived to take Gayle to a movie. But instead of his usual jeans and motorcycle jacket, he was wearing trousers, a cloth coat and regular street shoes. What's more, his beard was shaved off and his hair neatly trimmed.

"Don, you look great!" I exclaimed.

"Oh, I thought it was time for a change," he answered casually. But I knew Don was maturing and growing more self-assured, at the same time as he was deepening in his love for Gayle.

The following month—it was Christmas Eve, 1970—Don and Gayle announced their engagement. Marilyn and I had the privilege the same night of praying with Don to commit his life to the Lord Jesus. What a happy occasion it was! The evening ended up in a prayer meeting, as we all thanked God for His goodness.

Later, Gayle asked if her four "sisters" could be in the wedding. I was delighted—until one snowy evening several weeks later, when the Lord taught me a lesson about trusting Him.

Marilyn had roasted a succulent rib of beef, I remember, and the whole house was fragrant with the smell of it. Gayle and the four girls—Marty, Judy, Jeanne and Joni—had been out all afternoon, and it was beginning to snow. Suddenly the front door opened and all five of them burst in excitedly, stamping snow off their shoes.

"Come in and sit down," said Marilyn. "Why are you so late? We've been holding supper." I had already begun to carve the roast.

"Our dresses—we got them!" exclaimed Marty and Judy at the same time.

"What dresses?" asked Marilyn. I was concentrating on my carving.

"The dresses for the wedding," explained Gayle. "We put them on layaway. Wait till you see them!"

I looked up. "How much are they?"

"They're $69 each," said Judy, "but they're beautiful, Dad. You're going to love them."

"I didn't even let her finish. "Sixty-nine dollars each? For four dresses? You've got to be kidding!" Ignoring the warning look in Marilyn's eyes I blurted on, "We don't have that kind of money. You girls will have to forget about being in the wedding, that's all there is to it."

Once again I was focusing on the economic side of the situation, forgetting all about the riches of our heavenly Father.

But Marilyn hadn't forgotten. She was staring at me with disbelief and consternation. Four of the girls rushed from the table in tears. But Jeanne stayed behind long enough to exclaim, "You ought to be ashamed of yourself! Just when Gayle needs a family most, you're trying to take it away from her!" And she too flounced from the table and stormed up the stairs.

I didn't know what to say. The food was cold by this time, and I wasn't a bit hungry. Marilyn and I sat without a word.

Finally she said, "They're right, Bill Bair. You're not really thinking about the wedding at all. What you're thinking about is dollar signs. Don't you know the Lord will send us the money we need? He always has before."

I felt terrible, and I knew Marilyn was right. "Lord Jesus, will you forgive me?" I whispered.

Then I knew what else I had to do. Excusing myself from the table, I went upstairs. As I stood outside of Marty's room I heard voices.

"We still have two months before the wedding," Gayle was saying, "and I have a little money saved from my job."

"I can save my lunch money," Joni added, "and if we do some extra babysitting we can save a few dollars more each week."

I didn't wait to hear any more, but tapped lightly on the door. All five girls looked up in surprise.

"Girls, I need to ask your forgiveness," I said. "I know God is going to help us come up with the money for every one of those dresses. You're all going to look beautiful! I'm sorry I got angry."

What a time of forgiving and crying and hugging there was that night! It ended up in another prayer meeting, as we thanked God for each other and asked Him to meet all the expenses of Gayle's wedding.

In the next two months, the girls saved their money from babysitting and odd jobs. A friend contributed $100. Marilyn and I put in what we could. And by the time Gayle and Don were married the following Eastertime, God had supplied every penny.

Gayle and Don live nearby; they have a daughter who is six now. Every time we visit together I praise God for the miracle of accepting love that frees a young person from a pattern of rejection and offers a life of fulfillment and hope.

There are so many other miracles that have happened since

then. Let me tell you the story of our new house, and the headquarters for our work.

Things were busy at the foundation in the summer of 1969. Our work was expanding, and we were just meeting our daily operating costs with nothing left over.

In August I got a phone call from Sam Haines, the real estate agent in New Wilmington, telling me about a house that was for sale. He felt it would be perfect for our work.

"We're not thinking about a new house right now, Sam," I said. "Why? How much are they asking?"

"Sixty-thousand dollars."

I almost choked. "That might as well be $600,000! There's no way we could afford that."

But Sam said simply, "Come with me and see the place, Bill."

So I went. The Campbell Estate was reputed to be the nicest place in town, and after looking through the house with Sam I could see why. I loved everything about it, right down to its four acres of property and private, spring-fed lake. But the financing of it required more faith than I had.

Then I remembered the Old Testament story of Joshua, who walked around the city of Jericho seven times with the children of Israel and claimed its conquest for the Lord of hosts. God rewarded their faith with victory over the city.

I figured I didn't have anything to lose. So I excused myself from Sam and went for a walk around the lake.

"I'm stepping out in faith, Lord," I said aloud, "just like Joshua. And I claim this piece of property for Your work and for the Bair Foundation."

Then I thanked Sam and went home.

A month later Sam called to tell me the house had been sold. *So much for that,* I thought to myself. I felt disappointed, but I put the house—and my claim of faith—out of my mind.

Two years passed. God expanded our counseling staff, and we continued to trust Him for everyday needs. Our white clapboard house on Neshannock Avenue, for example, required so much paint that I could afford to cover only one side per year. That way the whole house got a fresh coat of paint every four years.

One day in September 1971, God spoke to Marilyn as she was praying. *Clean up the house, Marilyn,* He said to her. *It's going to be sold.*

Marilyn was thrilled, and she went to work that same day. But when she told me later what the Lord had said, I didn't fully share her enthusiasm. How could we afford to buy another house? And I didn't think too much more about it.

Two weeks later I got another call from Sam Haines, the realtor.

"Say, Bill, the Campbell Estate is on the market again," he said.

My heart jumped. "What's the selling price now?"

"Well, the new owner has put in some improvements, including $6,000 worth of carpeting. He's asking $68,000."

I couldn't help laughing. "Sam, if we couldn't afford $60,000 two years ago, what makes you think we can afford $68,000 now?"

It's so ideal for your work with the kids," he replied. "Why don't you come out and see the house again? And bring Marilyn along this time."

If anything, Marilyn loved the place even more than I had. Everything about it was perfect for us—except the price. We returned home exhilarated, but aware that the house was far out-of-reach financially.

In the middle of October I was painting the side of the house before the weather turned cold, when God spoke to me on the ladder 20 feet off the ground.

*Paint the whole house, Bill,* He said. *You're going to sell it.*

I almost fell off the ladder! It was the same message He had given to Marilyn, but what house did He have in mind for us to buy? Surely not the Campbell place! I had claimed it more than two years before, but we didn't even have money enough to buy the paint for this one.

Then I got a phone call from the president of a foundation in Philadelphia. He had just read some of our literature, he said, and wanted to come to Wilmington to see our work first hand. He arrived the next week with their attorney, explaining that their foundation was responsible for selecting a charitable organization every year into which to channel funds. Was there any particular piece of real estate we were interested in?

My jaw dropped, and I told him about the Campbell Estate. They went out with me to see it and left without saying another word about it.

Then on December 22, 1971, the vice-president of the foundation came for a personal visit and handed me a check for the down payment of $20,000, promising to pay off the rest of the house in three years.

How we praised God! For years our kids had clamored about how much they wanted a swimming pool, and now the Lord had given them their own private lake!

But then, our kids have always said that their heavenly Father gives them far more than their earthly father ever could. Take the time our three youngest daughters all needed winter coats. Marilyn and I didn't know where the money would come from. Then we got a call from Alice Moore, a Christian shopkeeper downtown.

"I was praying," she told us, "and the Lord seemed to be telling me to provide for your clothing needs. Well, I've sold all but three of my winter coats, and the Lord told me to give them to you. Could you use three women's leather coats?"

Could we! Those coats fit our girls as if they had been made for them—which we figured they had—and not so much as a hem ever needed to be altered.

"Thank God, Dad!" Jeanne told me later. "We're so glad you've introduced us to our heavenly Father. We get things much faster from Him, and we get better things."

That was the truth! Those leather coats were worth $100 each, while I had always bought imitation plastic with a fit looking three years ahead. But God wants the very best for us, right down to clothing that looks and fits great. And you know, Alice Moore has kept Marilyn and the girls clothed beautifully ever since.

In February 1972 the Bair family moved into our new home. But before long, word began filtering back that it wasn't "fitting" for the founder of a faith organization to live in such a nice house. The girls overheard critical remarks from teachers at school, and friends reflecting the comments of their parents. Some people in town were cool. Marilyn and I even received admonitions directly from Christian brothers and sisters that we sell the house and give the proceeds to the poor.

The criticism hurt Marilyn more than it did me, and she got so depressed that after a while she didn't even want to leave the house. One evening we were visiting some acquaintances, and Marilyn innocently read aloud an advertisement from the newspaper that seemed so ridiculous she found it humorous. It read, "How to get rich from other people's money."

"You're doing a real good job of that," muttered someone in a sarcastic voice.

Marilyn was crushed. Later that night she poured her heart out before the Lord.

"They don't understand what we're trying to do, Lord," she cried.

Then Marilyn heard the still, small voice of the Lord speaking to her. *I know, Marilyn,* He said. *They didn't understand what I was doing, either.*

Toward the end of 1975, we had been in our new home nearly four years. Our youngest daughter, Joni had graduated from high school, and Marilyn and I were traveling a good deal, sharing with groups and churches the work of the love homes,

The foundation, meanwhile, was outgrowing its offices on the second floor of the Globe Printing Building, and we believed God was leading us to build our own headquarters on the property next to the house. So an architect drew up the plans; the projected cost was $361,000. We knew that if God had given us the go-ahead, He would also provide the necessary funds.

In February 1976, the Lord spoke to me early one morning. *Bill,* He said, *when that building is completed, it's going to be paid for.* And He told me to request a two-year loan from the bank.

Two days later the Lord added that I should tell everyone boldly what He had promised—that the building would be paid for when it was finished.

We broke ground for the new building in March, and everywhere Marilyn and I went we shared with people God's wonderful promise. Others were as excited as we were, and as they contributed, a building fund grew.

In six months, construction had made good headway. By September the shell of the building was complete, and we moved in. Construction continued around us, and we made it through the first winter with small electric space heaters to keep warm.

But we were still nearly $200,000 short of our goal. Had I really heard the Lord? I began to wonder.

At the monthly meeting of the Board of Directors, one member expressed what was on everyone's mind.

"We know that God is eventually going to send us enough to pay for our new building," he said. "But maybe it's time to stop telling everyone that it's going to be paid for when it's completed. We're going to look ridiculous!"

Everyone reluctantly agreed. A little more discretion seemed sensible from a human standpoint; and, after all, no one was ruling out the possibility that a miracle would yet occur.

So for a month, Marilyn and I shared with people everything but what the Lord had instructed—and I was miserable. It seemed that the very bricks of our new building were crying out, "We'll be paid for!"

Then, at our next Board meeting, I had to speak out. "The Lord has given us a condition to meet," I said. "He told me plainly that the building will be paid for when it's completed, but at the same time we're to tell people what He had promised. Anything short of that is disobedience."

The agreement was unanimous. So again we began to declare openly the wonderful promise God had given us.

In February 1977 we were still more than $150,000 short. Marilyn and I were speaking on behalf of the Bair Foundation at a church in Norwalk, Ohio and I met for lunch with a Christian brother and successful businessman. Stan Bradley was a friend and generous contributor to the foundation, and as we lunched I filled him in on what God was doing. Then I gave him a progress report on our new headquarters.

"You know, Stan," I added, "the Lord promised me that when the building is finished, it's going to be completely paid for."

"Really?" asked Stan. "What's the balance on your building loan?"

"$164,000."

"Praise God!" he exclaimed. "I'll pray with you on that." And he picked up the tab for lunch.

Two months went by. In April Marilyn and I were back in Norwalk, and I gave Stan another call for lunch—on me this time. We met for hot roast beef sandwiches, as Stan related how God was taking care of details in his business.

Then, halfway through the meal, God laid a heavy one on me: *Ask Stan how much he's planning to contribute to the foundation for the rest of the year.*

I nearly choked on my salad. "Lord, I can't ask him that!" I protested silently.

But the conversation had paused, and I knew that God was holding the door open for me. Finally I looked up.

"Say, Stan," I said a little nervously, "can I ask you a personal question?"

"Sure thing," he replied.

"Well, I realize you've already given $5,000 to the foundation this year. But I was wondering—" I hesitated. "How much more are you planning to give?"

Stan looked as though he couldn't believe his ears. I was kind of hoping we'd both be raptured! But suddenly he started to smile.

"Funny you should ask," he said. "In fact, you're not going to believe this, Bill. But after we met for lunch a couple months ago, and you told me about your new building, I knew God wanted me to pay for it. But I told Him, 'I don't have the money to pay for it!' And He said, *Yes you do. Sell those duplexes.* I said, 'But, Lord, they're for my retirement.' And He said, *You take care of My business, and I'll take care of your retirement.*"

Stan took a bite of his roast beef sandwich. "Then I told the Lord that if He really wanted me to sell my duplexes, He'd have to arrange for you and me to get together again, and for you to ask me about contributing. Well, it looks like He's done that, doesn't it?"

I shot right out of my seat. "Praise the Lord!" I shouted. I didn't care if everyone in the restaurant heard me.

Stan put the duplexes on the market, at a selling price of

$164,000. In three months they hadn't sold, and I got a call from him.

"Maybe it wasn't the Lord," he said "I'll tell you what. I can give you a flat sum of $10,000 and handle monthly payments for the balance of the loan."

But that didn't sit right with me. "Let's give it a couple more weeks, Stan," I said. "If the duplexes haven't sold, we'll go ahead with our plan."

Stan and I did a lot of praying in the next two weeks. Then he gave me another call.

"Bill, I can't believe it!" he exclaimed. "I felt God wanted me to raise the asking price to $184,000—and do you know what? The duplexes just sold!" God had only wanted Stan to have a little extra.

In July 1978 the entire building was finished, including some modification and enlargement on the original structure. The same month Stan made the final payment on the original loan. Praise the Lord! He did just what He said He would do. And in a little more than ten years our administrative offices had expanded from a six-by-six room off our living room, to the basement of our garage, to some rooms in the Globe Printing Building, to a brand-new building of our own.

One of the reasons, I believe, is that God gives His children what they speak in faith ahead of time. The Lord has shown me the importance of what we confess with our mouth. Listen to what Jesus says in Mark 11:23: "Truly, I say unto you, whoever says to this mountain, 'Be taken up and cast into the sea,' and does not doubt in his heart, but believes that what he says will come to pass, it will be done for him."

I take that mountain to mean whatever unbelief we have in our hearts. If we cast it into the sea—where we "see" it no more—we will have whatever we ask for. The recognition of this simple truth has changed my vocabulary, because I believe that "what you say is what you get." The problem with many

Christians is that they are reaping the results of the negative talk that comes out of their mouths.

We have seen this time and time again in our work with teenagers. A youngster may be called a "lazy good-for-nothing" or "clumsy oaf" so often that he comes to believe it and act it out—and his parents have actually spoken it into being.

This is just one of the reasons I am concerned for the survival of the family. I have long believed that the family unit is the most important structure in our society, and the basic building block of the Body of Christ. At the same time, I recognize that the family in America today is under attack from Satan, from demonic forces, and from the rising tides of secularism and materialism.

The principles governing a Christ-centered family are basic and absolutely essential. They include the relevance of Scripture; the importance of listening to one another and to God; the value and uniqueness of every member of the family; and the importance of articulating family purposes and goals.

Neglecting any one of these principles will hinder a family from enjoying its full growth and unity in the Lord Jesus—as Marilyn and I discovered through a crisis that threatened to break up our marriage.

In the spring of 1978, a problem was developing in the office. I was receiving a growing volume of correspondence from friends and contacts of the foundation—many of whom Marilyn and I knew personally—which needed a personal reply. Yet writing has been a weak area of mine ever since my school days back in Altoona, and my schedule was demanding. As a result, the job simply wasn't getting done.

Also, since the administrative offices had moved next door, I sensed something wrong between Marilyn and me. Since our own children were nearly grown, and since we were on the road nearly half the time, few of the foundation kids came through our home anymore. But even when we were home, Marilyn hardly ever attended our 8:30 AM staff devotions as she used to, and she began finding excuses to stay away from special foundation get-togethers.

When we were on the road, traveling to speaking engagements, conversation about our work often grew tense and irritable. Disagreements left both of us wondering how we could speak in front of a group of people.

One summer evening Marilyn and I went out for dinner. Halfway through the meal, she voiced criticism of one of the staffers at the foundation. That was unlike her, but when I defended the person, our conversation turned into an argument.

Suddenly Marilyn grabbed her purse and left the table in a huff. When I followed her out to the parking lot, she didn't even let me hold open the car door for her. The ride home was quiet.

I began to choose my words carefully when talking about the foundation. Then I began avoiding the subject altogether. When Marilyn asked what was going on at the office, and I told her, she responded with increasing irritation—and sometimes downright anger.

I realized that Satan was trying to place a wedge between Marilyn and me and break up the work that God had begun. But, although we both recognized a growing problem, we felt powerless to do anything about it.

Then, after Marilyn and I had another argument one evening, I cried out, "Lord do something!" And God began to pave the way for healing.

The Lord led Marilyn and me to attent a Marriage Encounter weekend and we learned much through the experience.

The Lord showed me some areas I needed to work on, including listening to people in a way I hadn't done before. I began learning to minister to people's feelings, instead of running them over with my own feelings and ideas. This new lesson in communication began in my relationship with Marilyn.

God had given Marilyn and me a tremendous amount of compassion and understanding for the kids He brought into our lives, but neither one of us had much formal education. Marilyn was often defensive of me and self-conscious about her own high school diploma.

One warm evening in August, Marilyn and I were having coffee out on the patio. The lake was beautiful that night, but there was still tension between us and I felt the ache of frustration and helplessness about our lack of communication. I wanted to minister to Marilyn's feelings—to make her know how important she was—but I didn't know how.

"What can I do, Lord?" I pleaded silently.

Then the answer came back: *Ask her if she'd like a desk in your office.*

*A desk in my office?* I thought blankly. Then I was struck by the solution. Marilyn was the ideal person to handle that correspondence for the foundation! It seemed so obvious. She knew many of the individuals personally, and had such a gift for writing that I had often wished for a regular outlet for it. At the same time, Marilyn was too modest and unassuming to propel herself into a position of responsibility without specific encouragement from me.

Here was my opportunity. With a silent prayer of thanksgiving, I said, "Marilyn, how would you feel about having a desk in my office?"

She broke into a laugh, and turned to face me in her deck chair. "What would I do with a desk in your office?"

"Honey, you remember how overwhelmed we've been with all that personal correspondence at the foundation. Well, it just struck me that you're the perfect person to take care of it. As a matter of fact, there's an entire office available that you could have to yourself. And what a great opportunity for you to get involved again! I've missed you."

Marilyn didn't say anything for a minute. Then she looked at me. "Do you know what, Bill?"

"What?"

"I love you."

The following Monday morning Marilyn joined me for 8:30 staff devotions. As we gathered in a circle in the lounge to pray, Marilyn and I squeezed hands. She was back where she belonged.

Afterwards she headed down the hall toward her new office. There were five or six staffers clumped in front of the door—smiling, as she thought, a little suspiciously. After a few minutes of casual conversation, one of them said, "Aren't you going inside?"

Marilyn looked into the door. There, on the desk, was a flower arrangement with a note:

*We're so excited; happy, too!*
*They've made a permanent place for you!*
*So here's a welcome home bouquet*
*To our First Lady—hip, hip, hooray!*

"You don't know what that did for me, Bill," Marilyn told me later. "I had felt so left out and depressed. I was afraid I no longer had a part in the work. But if I had felt out-of-it before, now I feel more a part of things than ever!"

I praise God for Marilyn, and for each person connected with the love homes. Every single one has a unique role to play, whether they're foster dads and moms, counselors, administrators, fanner bees, supporters or secretaries. But if I had to single out an individual who has been the backbone of the organization, it would have to be Dr. Ada Peabody.

Ada was a member of Neshannock Presbyterian Church who, in 1967, came forward to support me in prayer; and she has been praying ever since. She now has some 80 fanner bees who "purify the air" of the Bair Foundation by praying regularly, by name, for each child and each foster family.

In addition, prayer volunteers donate a morning or afternoon each week to spend in our Prayer Room, interceding on behalf of specific needs and requests. Someone is in there most of the time, praying for the love homes and for the hundreds of requests that are sent in from all over the country. The power that comes from the Lord as a result of these prayers, and from the prayers of people throughout the United States, is the spiritual foundation for everything we do.

I've also learned much about the power of Satan and our authority as believers over him, ever since that busy Christmas when Barbara was delivered from the spirits of witchcraft and suicide. Time after time, the exercise of this authority has proven to be the turning point in the life of one of our kids or the answer to some particularly plaguing problem.

One of these problems, for me, has been the fear of not meeting our financial commitments. Despite the fact that God has never failed to supply our needs in the 11 years since I quit my job at the gas company, I have been subject to feats that the foundation is going to flounder.

Once I recognized these fears as an attack from the enemy, Marilyn and I purchased cassette tapes of the New Testament and began listening to them as went to sleep every night. Our spirits were strengthened by the reading of God's Word; and, in the morning, we joined in spiritual warfare, ordering Satan in the name of Jesus to keep his hands off our home, our children and all the homes where the love of Jesus is shared.

In many homes today, parents are so preoccupied—or have come from such inadequate homes themselves—that they are unable to give their children the love they need. These kids are looking for someone to love them regardless of what they do, and for someone to accept them just as they are.

Ron and Greg were looking for this kind of love. Ron was a street-wise kid from Brooklyn, one of 11 children. He had been in and out of trouble for most of his 14 years, and had been involved in a number of major crimes, including car theft with his older brother. When he was referred to the Bair Foundation in 1974 from a reformatory in upstate New York, Ron described his problems as "robbin' people, figntin' people and bein' in gang wars."

Greg was another product of a broken home. He, too, had been in trouble with the law—his specialty was burglary—and he, too, had spent a year in the reformatory. Greg couldn't allow himself to express his hurt and anger outwardly, so he kept it bottled up inside, along with all the pain of his 15 years of life.

We placed both boys in the home of Pete and Ethel Franklin, a black couple from nearby New Castle, Pa., who have love enough for their own eight children and plenty to spare. The Franklins had a growing interest in the work of the foundation. Ethel is warm and outgoing, and Pete is such a firm yet gentle father that we knew they were just the right family.

We weren't a bit surprised when good reports began to come back. Ron and Greg adjusted well to their new life. Despite some ups and downs, they made friends, improved in their schoolwork, went out for football, and became involved at church. Both boys committed their lives to Jesus Christ.

A year-and-a-half later, in the fall of 1975 a nearby hospital reported a minor case of vandalism, and the school officials suspected Ron and Greg. Some residents of New Castle took the opportunity to criticize the Franklins for having taken "deliquent" teenagers into their home. The foundation also received criticism. Pete and Ethel wondered if they should continue as a love home, or if Ron and Greg should be placed somewhere else.

Geert Steenwyk and another counselor spent time with the Franklins, talking through the problems and asking for God's clear guidance. It seemed to all of them that He was saying, "Keep the boys."

Two weeks later, the Franklins' world fell apart. It started one Sunday afternoon in October, as Ron was walking home from a friend's house. When he passed a new car lot, he admired a brand-new Oldsmobile parked in the front. Something seemed to tell him to check inside the car for the keys.

Ron resisted the temptation and continued walking. Three blocks later the suggestion came to him stronger than before: *The keys are in the glove compartment.* This time Ron gave in. He headed back to the lot at a brisk pace, and with a few furtive glances around, slipped into the passenger's side of the Oldsmobile. There, in the glove compartment, were the keys.

Ron was behind the wheel before he knew it. The powerful engine roared into life, and he drove out of the lot and into downtown New Castle. He felt as though he were back in Brooklyn, on some job with his older brother, with the months since that time some kind of dream.

A problem brought him back to the present: How to get the car back into the lot without being seen? It didn't seem as easy as it had been to steal the car, somehow; and besides, after reflection, Ron wasn't sure he was ready to return it yet. So he parked it on a side street near home for the night, and attended the evening service at church as if nothing had happened.

The next morning Ron drove "his" car to school. During the day he filled Greg in on what he had done, and when school let out, Ron and Greg cut football practice and went for a drive. Unknown to both boys, the owner of the car lot had notified the police.

As Ron and Greg cruised past a rival school, looking for friends to impress, a police car caught sight of the Olds and signalled to the boys to pull over. But Ron panicked. Instead of stopping, he followed an instinct drilled into him from years of experience: *If the cops come, run.* And he peeled away.

"Ron stop!" shouted Greg. "You're crazy!" But Ron had lost his head, and there was no stopping him.

The police chased the car through the streets of New Castle, sirens wailing, weaving through rush-hour traffic.

Then the inevitable happened: Ron ran a red light. Halfway through the intersection, he hit a Cadillac broadside. As both cars careened, Ron lost control. His car jumped the curb, hit a woman pedestrian and crashed into a store.

The Franklins and I met at the emergency room in a state of shock. Both boys were injured, but the pedestrian and the driver of the other car—a woman in her 40s—were in critical condition. Relatives stood around in tense groups, awaiting news of their loved ones, and policemen were waiting to take Ron and Greg into custody.

Right there in the waiting room we did the only thing we could do: We huddled in a tight little circle and prayed for God's mercy. Minutes later, we learned that the driver of the Cadillac was dead.

Pete and Ethel Franklin were beside themselves with guilt and remorse. Had they misunderstood God's leading just two weeks before? If only they had given Ron and Greg up, perhaps this never would have happened.

No one got much sleep that night. And the next morning, we received another call from the hospital: The woman pedestrian had just died.

Seldom have I been more despondent, with profound doubts for the very survival of the Bair Foundation. There had been sufficient criticism of our work that I was afraid this would turn the tide against us, and that our charter would be revoked.

*It's all over*, I thought. *This is the end of the foundation.*

We did a lot of praying that day; and as we prayed, God reminded us of a passage of Scripture: "For we know that all things work together for good to them that love God, to them who are the called according to His purpose" (Rom. 8:28). We believed we had been called according to His purpose, but it was hard to understand how a tragedy like this could be turned to good for anyone.

I began to find out the very next night. It was pouring rain as I drove to the funeral home to pay our respects to the family of the woman driver. I have never been at more of a loss to know what to say.

There were flowers all over the room, and maybe 15 people

there by the time I arrived. Most were relatives, I guessed, but I recognized the middle-aged husband from the emergency room two nights before. He stood with his daughter next to the casket, and I saw that they both had been crying.

"I'm Bill Bair, " I said quietly. "I just wanted to tell you how sorry I am, and offer to do anything I can to help."

The man looked at me with no trace of hostility or bitterness—just sorrow. My heart went out to him. Suddenly his daughter began to cry.

"We know about your work, Mr. Bair," she said. "My mom was a Christian, and so am I."

My spirit leaped. "Would you mind if I prayed with you?"

"I wish you would," replied her father. "I don't have much faith myself, but I could sure use some about now." Tears welled in his eyes.

So we drew close, putting our arms around one another. The Lord gave us a few minutes free from interruptions, as I asked that the God of all comfort put His arms around this grieving family and enfold them in His love.

As we prayed, I sensed the Lord's presence in a special way, enveloping and comforting us. When I finished praying, the daughter was smiling, and her father and I shared a warm embrace. I left the funeral home rejoicing in the Lord's goodness and praising Him for the healing I knew had already begun.

It took time. Months followed of complicated legal proceedings for Ron and Greg. The local newspapers jumped on the story, displaying it on their front pages. Pete and Ethel Franklin came in for a lot of adverse publicity, and entered a period of deep discouragement, wondering at the wisdom of continuing in their work with teenagers.

Then God showed Pete and Ethel a passage of Scripture that especially encouraged them. It was Matthew 8:23-27, in which Jesus and His disciples encountered a storm on the Sea of Galilee. Jesus admonished the disciples for their lack of faith.

But then He quieted the storm; and when they reached the other side, Jesus' ministry flourished.

"We're not jumping out of the boat now," Pete and Ethel decided. "We want to reach the other side."

The incident gradually strengthened their resolve that they had done right in deciding to keep Ron and Greg.

"In the middle of that whole situation," Ethel told me later, "I learned for the first time what it means to forgive—forgive the boys, and the other people too—and something of what it must have cost Jesus to say, 'Father, forgive them.'"

"I learned just how much of love is really commitment," added Pete. "When someone hurts you, as Ron and Greg hurt us, you want to withdraw. But we had made a commitment to those boys, and we learned how strong our love through the Lord could be."

Ron was detained for several months before being sentenced in the same reformatory he had stayed at more than a year before. Pete and Ethel were allowed to visit him just before Christmas.

"The first time we saw him," says Pete, "things just began to break up in me. I knew he was still my son, and that it didn't matter what he had done. I realized, too, that we needed him just as much as he needed us. He was our son, and nothing could ever change that."

The court finally ruled that Ron could not return to the Franklins, so he was sent back to his home in Brooklyn. He still lives there, and has a steady job. Ron just turned 18, and is now free to come and visit the Franklins.

Greg was not allowed to return to New Castle, either. He was assigned to another foster home, but he ran away to the Franklins. then he was returned to his mother, while details were being worked out for his return to the Franklins. But he had fallen so far behind in his schoolwork, and felt so guilty about the accident, that he decided voluntarily to remain in his hometown. Greg is now studying auto body repair, and maintains contact with the Franklins.

Pete and Ethel are now committed firmly to the work of the love homes, and have taken nine more foundation kids into their own home since the accident.

"We need all our foster kids," says Pete, "the more the better. We're not whole without them."

What has happened to some of the other kids who have been part of our lives? Shirley is married now, and has a beautiful baby girl. She and her husband live in Toronto, where she is secretary at the headquarters of the Full Gospel Business Men's Fellowship International.

Barbara is a practical nurse at a hospital in Rochester, N.Y., and visits us a couple times a year. Herbert is a corporal in the U.S. Army and doing very well.

Jeff's is a sadder story. We hadn't heard from Jeff for several years, until Marilyn got a burden of prayer for him recently. Then Geert received word that Jeff had run away from home and hitchhiked to California, where be became involved with heavy drugs. Now he is in a mental hospital, and the prognosis is not good.

Our son Ted and his wife, Chris, have three boys—6, 5 and 3. Marty and her husband, John Horrigan, are the parents of two boys, 5 and 2. Judy is working for two chiropractors nearby and shares an apartment with Laura, one of the counselors from the foundation. Jeanne is ready to graduate from college with a degree in physical education and health, and looks forward to a career in teaching. Our youngest, Joni, is married to Ken Knechtel and works as a secretary at the foundation. John and Bea Love bought a farm outside Altoona where they are involved full-time in prisoner rehabilitation.

Our staff at the foundation has grown since early days. As of early 1979, we employed a staff of 20 full-time counselors, administrative personnel, and secretaries; and the number of love homes has grown steadily along with the number of boys and girls placed in them.* But when all the figures are added up, all the budgets formulated, and all the plans for tomorrow laid out, we can never get away from our focus on the individual child and his family. It takes only a handful of kids whose stories have happy endings to remind us that everything we do is centered around people.

One of these kids is Mark. His parents were separated when he was young. Mark was a bright, good-looking boy who learned early how to manipulate people to get what he wanted, and he knew how to use his intelligence and good looks to satisfy a compulsive need for attention.

When Mark was nine, he set fire to his toybox to get attention from his mother. Throughout grade school he feigned attacks of illness to get sent home from school. By the time Mark was 12, stealing and lying had become a serious problem, so his mother sent him to live with his aunt and uncle. While there, he prayed at a Baptist church to receive Jesus as his Savior. But severe problems persisted, and in May 1974, the county referred him to us.

We knew Mark needed a warm, accepting home where he would receive love and discipline, and parents who could hold out against his manipulative abilities. Mark had never had a stable adult male to relate to, and he needed a compassionate mother who could give him the affection he had never known.

Then we thought of the Macks. Joan Mack was John Love's youngest daughter, a member of the original "Love home." Joan had inherited from John and Bea Love a burden for the work of the foundation; and her husband, Bill, was such a loving father yet firm disciplinarian with their own two youngsters that we felt they would provide just the guidance and stability Mark needed. When they agreed eagerly to receive Mark into their home, we felt the circle of love homes was complete.

*See Appendix

Mark was 14 when he went to live with the Macks, but the bright, manipulative adolescent brought more problems than Bill and Joan knew how to handle. He was failing at school, and even altered his first report card. Every night became a confrontation with Bill as Mark refused to do his homework. Whenever Mark was left alone with the kids, one of them got hurt. When Bill wasn't around, Mark was disrespectful to Joan, sometimes abusing her verbally in front of her friends. Money turned up missing. And Mark lied habitually.

Bill tried paddling him a couple of times, with no noticeable improvement. Revoking privileges was little better. When Bill or Joan tried to talk with Mark, he would mutter sullenly, "I don't have anything to talk about." Yet with his friends and teachers, Mark was humorous and charming; and he put on friendly, affectionate displays with counselors from the foundation.

Then the Macks discovered that Mark had stolen a necklace from a store downtown and given it to a girl at school. Bill made him confess to the shopkeeper and save up money to pay for the necklace. But Bill and Joan were ready to give Mark up, and Joan called the foundation in tears.

One of our counselors, Janet Dibble, drove out to the Macks' the same afternoon.

"Bill and Joan were more uptight than I had ever seen them," Janet told me later. "Joan made coffee for us, and Bill sat down at the kitchen table looking like the picture of despondence."

"As we began to talk, they poured out all the frustrations and hurts of the last few months. They shared their growing sense of failure, and their inability to know what to do. They had tried everything, yet something seemed to be in the way—something we couldn't quite put our finger on."

"I just listened, my heart aching along with theirs. I didn't have any idea what to do."

So they prayed. We have found that when we run out of our

own worldly wisdom, God can move in with His wisdom from above—and Bill and Joan were in need of that wisdom now. Janet led out in a prayer.

"I asked the Lord to show us how to pray," Janet said later, "and I asked Him to show us specifically what He wanted us to do. I thanked Him for Mark, and for the Macks, and for the guidance He was going to give us. And then we just sat at the table, waiting."

"As we did, God began to show me a number of things. For one, He seemed to be saying that there wasn't something Bill and Joan were doing wrong, and that they shouldn't assume a false sense of failure or responsibility for Mark's behavior. That was important."

"Then the Lord began to show me that the problem was spiritual—that there was demonic influence at work in Mark that we needed to combat spiritually. I had learned a little about demonic oppression and the concept of spiritual warfare, but this was the first time I had sensed it so clearly. The Lord told me that this was a battle we needed to fight on Mark's behalf if he were to be free."

Everyone was still quiet. Finally Bill spoke up. "Did anyone hear anything from the Lord?" he asked.

"I did," said Janet. And then, "Are either of you familiar wth spiritual warfare, and the authority of the believer?"

Bill nodded. "A little. Go on."

"Well, while we were praying," continued Janet, "the Lord showed me that there's a spiritual battle going on over Mark, and that we need to stand for him against demonic powers that are harassing him. Before he can be free to be obedient—to you and to the Lord—he needs to be set free from the bondage he's under."

Bill got his Bible, and as they had more coffee they began to look up passages of Scripture. They were familiar with the one in Ephesians 6: "For we are not contending against flesh and blood, but against the principalities, against the powers, against the world rulers of this present darkness, against the spiritual hosts of wickedness in the heavenly places. Therefore take the whole armor of God..."

They also looked at Luke 9:1 "(Jesus) called the twelve together and gave them power and authority over all demons..." And Matthew 18:18, which Jesus addressed to His disciples and to the church: "Truly, I say to you, whatever you bind on earth shall be bound in heaven, and whatever you loose on earth shall be loosed in heaven."

When they closed the Bible, Joan said, "If there are demons that have been harassing Mark, how do we know which ones they are, to pray against them?"

So again they turned to the Lord, asking Him this time to reveal the spirits by name. After a period of silence, all three of them were impressed with some names. Bill got a pencil and wrote down *rejection, rebellion, lying, stealing* and *jealousy*.

"Since we have the authority over Satan and all his demons, according to the Word of God," said Janet, "we need to address those spirits by name, bind their power over Mark, and rebuke them in the name of Jesus from oppressing him."

"Bill you're head of the house and the spiritual authority over Mark," said Joan. "Why don't you pray, and we'll agree?"

The coffeepot was long empty. They pushed their cups and saucers aside, and joined hands around the table. Bill led them in a prayer.

"Lord Jesus," he said, "in Your name, and with Your authority, we bind the demons that have been harassing Mark—rejection, rebellion, lying, stealing and jealousy. And we ask You, Lord, to loose Your Holy Spirit in their place, and begin to do a new work in Mark's life."

When the were done praying, each felt a tremendous sense of relief. "The Lord had lifted every bit of heaviness from that table," said Janet, "and Bill and Joan looked more hopeful than they had in months."

They agreed to continue individually to bind those spirits from Mark every day for a week.

Then Joan spoke up. "You know, I feel a little reluctant to face Mark after some of the things he's said to me, and some of the ways I've responded. I wonder if God wants me to ask Mark's forgiveness."

"Why don't you, honey?" Bill replied. "It might be just the thing to open up your relationship with him, and pave the way for the Lord's healing."

Say a prayer!" said Joan. And as Janet began stacking dishes in the sink, Joan got Mark from his room and they went out the back door for a talk.

When they returned a half hour later, Mark's arm was around Joan's shoulder, and they had both been crying.

"How are you, son?" asked Bill.

"Better," replied Mark with a smile. "Lots better." Joan couldn't say a word. She was crying again.

That was the beginning of a new life for Mark. His schoolwork improved immediately. His relationship with the Mack children blossomed. He became more helpful around the house. The lines of communication with Bill and Joan opened up, and he began to get involved with the youth group at church.

That was all nearly four years ago. Mark is now a senior in high school, earning A's and B's. He was just accepted at a college outside of Pittsburgh, and was nominated recently for *Who's Who in American High Schools*. Joan reports that he sometimes leaves her a bouquet of flowers or a note, thanking her for being "such a terrific mom."

"Mark has come a long way," Joan told me the other day. "It was a struggle, but it's been worth it."

A struggle occurs in every family committed to share the love of Jesus with a boy or girl who has never known it before. It takes nothing less than the power of the Holy Spirit to love an alienated, unlovable kid until he begins to respond. The youngster will bring it to the test—sometimes over and over—to see if it will hold up. And only the agape love of Jesus can.

Because, when all is said and done, and when every story is accounted for, a ministry like ours ends up in the same place it began—with the love of Jesus. And the last chapter of that story has yet to be written.

# Since then . . .

Another five years have passed as we write these pages. We praise the Lord for the exciting ways that He has refined and expanded our ministry to so many troubled and unloved teenagers.

Marilyn and I were present at Oral Roberts University graduation ceremonies this past spring to see Mark, one of the teens we shared about previously, as he graduated from ORU. Mark wants to minister for Jesus as a full-time evangelist. Glory!!

Last year, The Bair Foundation went through a time where finances were tight and we sensed the Lord preparing to do a new work. Ron Brown, our executive vice-president, came into me one day and shared that he felt God had touched his heart about the need for an educational and training program to reach teens with really severe problems. It sounded like a great way to reach out and touch the lives of teens who really need to know the peace and victory that can be theirs through Jesus Christ. We had a building that would house the program and the Lord sent us, in Morris Kirk, the right person to develop the educational and training portion of the program.

The Lord was calling us to again step out in faith as we learned that the total cost of the program must be met through private contributions. We prayed and agreed to move forward. All of this happened as experts in the field of child care were saying that this was a time to cut back, not expand. But, the Lord was faithful as we moved ahead and soon there were a half a dozen teens enrolled in L.I.F.E. (Learning by Individualized Fundamental Education) Academy.

I know that the Lord has sent some teens with pretty tough problems to us in the past, but He was now sending us a real "hardcore" type of teen.

At times, we have had 16 to 18 students enrolled in L.I.F.E. Academy. Each has a moving story and we praise the Lord for the victory He has given us. Several of these incidents are still very vivid. . .

Like the young man who had come from a tough family situation and whose parents had divorced. As he grew up, his truancy and discipline problems in school became worse; add to that a low self-esteem and an inability to control anger and you have a walking time bomb!

As the staff sought the Lord for direction, all hell broke loose as Jerry lost all self-control and flipped out right in the hallway of our administration building. The spiritual battle became intense, and Satan literally overtook this young man. One of our caseworkers recalled, "It was a battle between Satan and Jesus. As Satan was confronted with the faith of deliverance of 6 men, he took over Jerry's body causing him to break an office chair and kick a hole in the wall. The voice coming from Jerry was cursing and mocking Jesus verbally, with frothing at the mouth. With red eyes bulging and filled with a hatred that was not from this world, one could see the rage coming from Jerry's eyes." Later, Marilyn told me she went into the mailing room tearfully pleading with God, and the Lord spoke to her heart saying, "The glory of the Lord shall be revealed."

At one point, Wes Fritz (our chief of maintenance) who is in his mid-70s with snow-white hair and small in build, stood toe-to-toe with Jerry, commanding Satan out in the name of Jesus. Fritz isn't small in stature with the Lord, and those ministering began to see Satan's hold of Jerry break.

In spite of the verbal lashing, Jerry wasn't able to even touch Fritz or any other staff member. The Lord only allows Satan so much control.

Jerry received his prayer language as he was ministered to after Satan was defeated. A prevalent comment from those participating in the deliverance was, "I never knew Satan hated Jesus so much." Jerry, bathed in perspiration, remembered nothing of what happened during the ordeal.

But the real miracle came when Jerry went home for a visit with his family a few weeks later and led other family members including his mom to the Lord!! Praise Jesus!!

Then there is Pat. Neglected by his mother, he was on his own most of the time as far back as he can remember. Deprived of what most of us take for granted, Pat would often scrounge a meal from a trash container that held the garbage that others had thrown away.

I remember the day he came to The Foundation with his worldly possessions — a half-filled paper bag of worthless clothing. While Pat is an intelligent young man, his actions were a challenge for the L.I.F.E. Academy staff. He stole food and hoarded pencils, tablets, and anything he could collect. Often he would act out in a variety of ways to receive negative attention and discipline, because he really believed that he was worthless, junk.

Although we have a teacher and an assistant for every five

students, Pat had to have an individual instructor for most of the school day. My daughter Jeanne (one of the teachers) relates about the day Gayne Bortz (another of the teachers) had a birthday, and some of the students baked and decorated a cake for her. As the students gathered in the game area to sing "happy birthday" and share the cake, Pat soon ended up sitting in the middle of the pool table downing his cake. His supply of sugar needs to be regulated due to hyperactivity. In the gaiety of the occasion, Pat had eaten several pieces of cake and had become beligerant and aggressive and was lashing out at anyone around him. His face changed and he started pounding with fists on anyone who happened to be near him.

But we praise the Lord that, shortly after he came to us, Pat met Jesus and discovered that "God don't make junk". There have been periods when Pat regressed to stealing, lying, and defiant behavior. But, as Pat has steadily grown in the Lord and has been taught about God's word, we have seen major improvements.

Pat enjoys working in wood shop and is constantly asking my staff if they want him to make something for them—for a special price!

Finally, let me say a few words about Nancy. She was one of the first teens to come to L.I.F.E. Academy and we wondered how the Lord would work to soften her heart. She was a street kid who was rebellious, angry with her parents, and very strong-willed. Coming from a big city, she hadn't attended school for a number of years and told us she would walk in one door at school in the morning. . . and immediately out the other.

Nancy was involved in both the alcohol and drug scene, although she wasn't addicted to either. She had completed a residential program prior to coming to The Bair Foundation. That provided a temporary solution, but progress made there didn't last and Nancy was sent to us.

In spite of Nancy's rocky family life, she was always very respectful to her foster parents. As we prayed and ministered to her, she accepted Jesus and the walls began to crumble. Nancy completed the L.I.F.E. Academy program and returned to a traditional school. I'm sure that school isn't the most exciting thing in Nancy's life. She still has problems because her years of skipping school put her far behind, but she is trying to do her best with the help of the Lord and her foster family.

I remember the day Nancy left L.I.F.E. Academy; she had softened alot, but still wanted to maintain a certain amount of a tough image. Nancy led the devotions that morning and at the close asked if she could share for a few minutes with the other "kids".

She began by stating that a personal relationship with Jesus—and the need to be in the Word and in prayer—weren't options for her or her classmates. "You need Jesus if you want to make it out there", she said emphatically, her eyes filling with tears.

Nancy confessed her fear of returning to a traditional school and then, her voice quivering, explained that the reason she had been so quiet the past few days was because she had been praying for each one of her classmates and teachers.

She encouraged the teens, "Get your act together with Jesus and start living for Him. And, start listening to these teachers. They really love us and care for us even when we don't do what they tell us to do".

The tears still flowing, this "street kid" went to her classmates and teachers and gave each a big hug. By this time, she wasn't the only one crying; there wasn't a dry eye in the room! Even the so-called real "tough, hard" teens had tears streaming or silently sliding down their cheeks.

Because the teens have such a need for acceptance and

reassurance of love, many times they act out in such negative ways seeking assurance that we can love them through any situation. There are some tough days here at L.I.F.E. Academy here at The Bair Foundation. We continue to share the love of Jesus with these teens, and every time there is a breakthrough and a victory like Jerry's, Pat's, or Nancy's, it is such a time of joy and an opportunity to praise our gracious Lord and Savior for His goodness and mercy.

We also rejoice that the Lord has caused us to grow to minister to teens from throughout eastern Ohio through most of Pennsylvania and into northern West Virginia.

And, we are excited about the way that the Lord is again opening a new door—this time to enable us to minister to the natural families of foster teens and to many families experiencing problems at a point prior to removal of the children and teens from the home.

The new program the Lord is developing is called ExODUS Experience and involves group task-solving in a way that the members of the group are drawn closer together as they must work together and depend on one another as they attempt to solve certain tasks. ExODUS stands for Experiential Opportunities Developing Unity and Success. I know that the Lord will reach out and touch many lives as families leave the bondage of a spiritual Egypt, travel through the wilderness, and arrive triumphantly in the Promised Land.

With this new means of sharing the love of Jesus comes new concerns and new obstacles as well as new ways for our wonderful Savior and Lord to manifest Himself in our presence